# Troy

## Archaeological Histories

*Series editor: Thomas Harrison*

An important series charting the history of sites, buildings and towns from their construction to the present day. Each title examines not only the physical history and uses of the site but also its broader context: its role in political history, in the history of scholarship, and in the popular imagination.

*Tarquinia*, Robert Leighton
*Avebury*, Joshua Pollard & Mark Gillings
*Pompeii*, Alison E. Cooley
*Ur*, Harriet Crawford

# Troy

## Myth, City, Icon

Naoíse Mac Sweeney

BLOOMSBURY ACADEMIC
LONDON • NEW YORK • OXFORD • NEW DELHI • SYDNEY

BLOOMSBURY ACADEMIC
Bloomsbury Publishing Plc
50 Bedford Square, London, WC1B 3DP, UK

BLOOMSBURY, BLOOMSBURY ACADEMIC and the Diana logo
are trademarks of Bloomsbury Publishing Plc

First published in Great Britain 2018

Cover design: Terry Woodley
Cover image © SZ Photo/Scherl/Bridgeman Images

A catalogue record for this book is available from the British Library.

Library of Congress Cataloging-in-Publication Data
Names: Mac Sweeney, Naoâise, 1982- author.
Title: Troy / Naoise Mac Sweeney.
Description: New York: Bloomsbury Academic, an imprint of Bloomsbury
Publishing PLC, 2018. | Series: Archaeological histories; 7 |
Includes bibliographical references and index.
Identifiers: LCCN 2017031722 | ISBN 9781472532510 (hardback) |
ISBN 9781472529374 (pbk.) | ISBN 9781472521774 (ePDK) |
ISBN 9781472522511 (ebook)
Subjects: LCSH: Troy (Extinct city) | Excavations (Archaeology)–Turkey–Troy
(Extinct city) | Turkey–Antiquities.
Classification: LCC DF221.T8 M18 2018 | DDC 939/.21–dc23
LC record available at https://lccn.loc.gov/2017031722

ISBN:   HB:  978-1-4725-3251-0
        PB:  978-1-4725-2937-4
     ePDF:  978-1-4725-2177-4
    eBook:  978-1-4725-2251-1

Series: Archaeological Histories

Typeset by Jones Ltd, London
Printed and bound in Great Britain

To find out more about our authors and books visit
www.bloomsbury.com and sign up for our newsletters.

# Contents

# List of Illustrations

## Maps

## Table

## Figures

# Acknowledgements

I began writing this book while on maternity leave with my eldest son, Gianni, and completed it when I was on maternity leave with my younger one, Valentino. This book is dedicated to them.

I owe a great debt to the people who made writing this book possible: first and foremost, my mother, Leong, and also my mother-in-law, Denise, and my aunt, Siew Lang, who took turns stepping into the childcare breach while I wrote. I am also grateful to Giselle Borg Oliver, Damjan Krsmanovic, Mortimer Mac Sweeney, John Vella, and John Nielsen for reading part or all of the manuscript while it was in preparation and for offering helpful pointers and suggestions.

Finally, I also owe thanks to Alice Wright and Clara Herberg at Bloomsbury for their input and guidance in preparing the book, as well as to Michael Hawkes and Tina Ross for the wonderful drawings, and to Michael Squire and the Metropolitan Museum of Art for permission to reproduce their images.

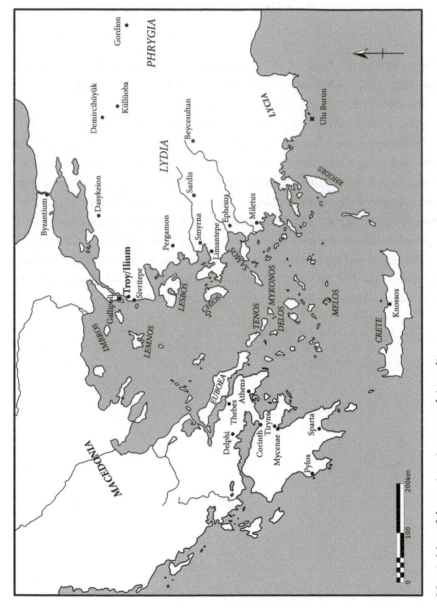

**Map 1** Map of the ancient Aegean and Anatolia.

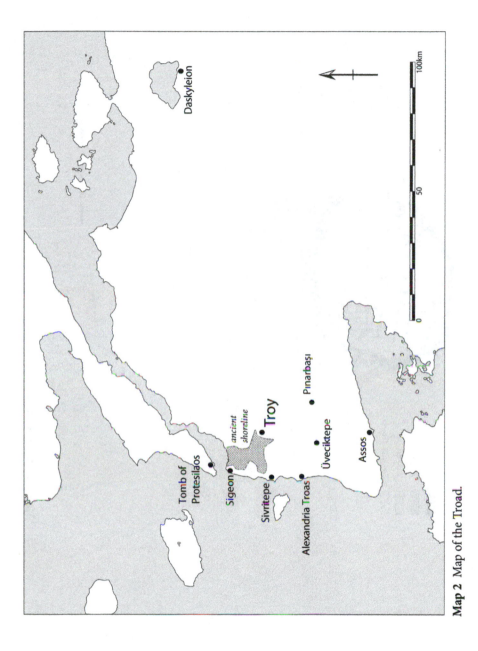

**Map 2**  Map of the Troad.

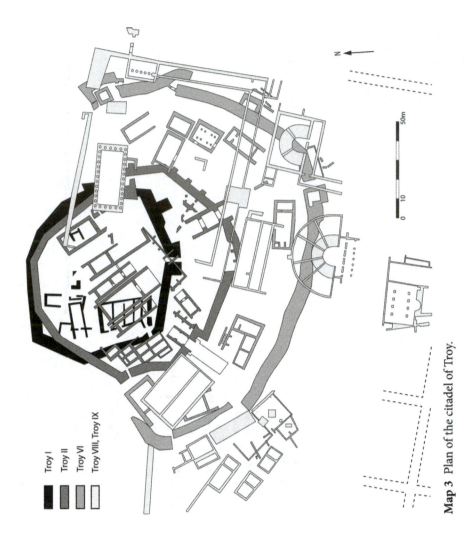

Troy I
Troy II
Troy VI
Troy VIII, Troy IX

50m

10

0

**Map 3** Plan of the citadel of Troy.

**Table 1** Chronological table

| | | |
|---|---|---|
| 3000 | Troy I | Early Bronze Age I: The spread of bronze working across the Near East; the beginnings of seafaring |
| 2900 | | |
| 2800 | | |
| 2700 | | |
| 2600 | | |
| 2500 | | |
| 2400 | Troy II | Early Bronze Age II: Urbanization, increased connectivity and trade around the Near East |
| 2300 | | |
| 2200 | Troy III | Early Bronze Age III: Growth of central Anatolian communities |
| 2100 | Troy IV | |
| 2000 | | |
| 1900 | Troy V | Middle Bronze Age: Old Assyrian Empire; increased trade across Near East; written records appear for Anatolia |
| 1800 | | |
| 1700 | Troy VI | Late Bronze Age: Complex states and empires; sophisticated networks of trade and diplomacy across Mediterranean and Near East; 'Age of Heroes' |
| 1600 | | |
| 1500 | | |
| 1400 | | |
| 1300 | Troy VIIa | |
| 1200 | | |
| 1100 | Troy VIIb | Early Iron Age: Greater fluidity and instability in political structures; emergence of Phoenician and Greek trade networks across the Mediterranean |
| 1000 | | |
| 900 | | |
| 800 | Troy VIII (Geometric) | The Greek World: Emergence of Homeric poetry; spread of Greek settlement across the Mediterranean; rise of aristocratic culture; Persian Wars; Athenian Empire and Peloponnesian War; campaigns of Alexander of Macedon; Hellenistic kingdoms |
| 700 | | |
| 600 | Troy VIII (Archaic) | |
| 500 | | |
| 400 | Troy VIII (Classical) | |
| 300 | | |
| 200 | Troy VIII (Hellenistic) | |
| 100 | | |

| | | |
|---|---|---|
| 0 | Troy IX (Roman) | The Roman World: Roman Republic and Julius Caesar; Augustus and the establishment of the Principate; continued spread of the Roman Empire; relocation of the imperial capital to Byzantium; split into the Eastern and Western Empires |
| 100 | | |
| 200 | | |
| 300 | | |
| 500 | | |
| 600 | | |
| 700 | Site mostly uninhabited | Medieval period: Knowledge of Homer restricted to scholars within the Byzantine Empire; Benoît and the composition of the Trojan romances; claiming of Trojan ancestry by European noble houses; Crusades; Chaucer; establishment of the Ottoman Empire |
| 800 | | |
| 900 | | |
| 1000 | | |
| 1100 | | |
| 1200 | | |
| 1300 | | |
| 1400 | | Renaissance: Rediscovery of Classical culture in western Europe; Tintoretto; export of European arts to China |
| 1500 | | |
| 1600 | | Early Modern Period: Shakespeare; Age of Exploration |
| 1700 | | |
| 1800 | | |
| 1900 | Excavations at Troy: Schliemann, Dörpfeld, Blegen, Korfmann | Modern Period: Nineteenth-century Orientalism; Gladstone; Gallipoli; Giraudoux; Seferis; Proença Filho; Heaney; Tom Waits; Joe Biden |
| 2000 | | |
| 2100 | | |

# Part One

# Myth

# 1

# Introducing Troy

Troy! It is a name to conjure with, a name which carries a rich tangle of associations, invoking stories, images, and ideals.

The unique fame of Troy comes from its myth – the myth of the Trojan War. It is a story best known from Homer's epic poem, the *Iliad*, composed in Ancient Greek in the eighth century BCE. The poem explores love and anger, duty and heroism, setting these against the dramatic backdrop of a bloody and ongoing war. This war was, of course, the decade-long conflict between the massed armies of the Achaean Greeks on one side and the Trojans and their allies on the other, resulting in the eventual defeat and destruction of Troy. Throughout history, the name of Troy has been synonymous with this myth of the Trojan War, and the story of Troy has always been bound up with the story of this conflict.

Behind the myth lay a real city of bricks and stone, inhabited by real people of flesh and blood. The city of Troy was a fully functioning community from the start of the Bronze Age until the seventh century CE, a period of almost four millennia. During this time, its fortunes waxed and waned. There were times when the city flourished, its population expanded, and its wealth multiplied. The Late Bronze Age, the Hellenistic period, and the Imperial Roman period were such moments. But there were other times when the city's fortunes plummeted and the number of its occupants dwindled. Such times included the Early Iron Age and the Byzantine period. Today, we divide the archaeological site of Troy into nine main chronological phases, Troy I–IX, to distinguish the remains of these different periods. The nine cities of Troy represent, in effect, the nine lives of a real community.

However, Troy is more than merely a city or a myth. It is also an idea – an abstract concept that resonates today just as it has resonated through the twenty-eight centuries that separate us from Homer. This idea extends beyond the individual city itself, or the specific legend of the Trojan War. It has resulted in Troy being depicted in works of literature and art across numerous countries and cultures, and deployed in popular culture for everything from computer programmes to condoms. In the present, as it has been in ages past, Troy is a cultural icon.

This book approaches Troy from these three different perspectives – through its myth, as an archaeological site, and as a cultural icon. The three are necessarily interdependent – the icon would not exist without the myth, the myth would not have endured without the city, and the city would not have developed along the particular trajectory that it did without being a cultural icon. All are crucial to our understanding and appreciation of what Troy fundamentally *is* and its significance through the centuries.

This book is not a guide to the archaeological remains at the site of Troy. Many such books already exist, and it is not my aim to duplicate the excellent publications which are already available. Nor is this book a comprehensive study of the story of the Trojan War and the way this story has endured and echoed through the centuries. Such a study would occupy far more time and space than is available between these slim covers. Rather, this book aims to offer a broad exploration of Troy through history. Its focus is Troy from the time of its first occupation in *c.* 3000 BCE until the present day, considering the reality of Troy as a city and community alongside its wider significance as a social and cultural symbol. By means of introduction, three brief vignettes will serve to illustrate its approach.

* * *

Scene 1. A lonely grave on a windswept shore. A young warrior kneels in front of a giant burial mound. In his hands, still wet with the blood of the sheep he has just sacrificed, he holds a wreath. He lays it at the foot of the tall grave stele. Behind him stands a vast army, keeping a respectful silence in the presence of their kneeling king. This king is the young Alexander of Macedon, visiting the tomb of Achilles at Troy on his way to meet the Persian army. It is said that Alexander lamented at Achilles' tomb, not just for the dead heroes of ages past, but that there was no Homer alive to chronicle his own great deeds (Arrian, *Anabasis* 1.11-12). But why did Alexander break off his pursuit of the Persian army to tour the remains of Troy, and to pay his respects to the dead heroes of the Trojan War? What would he have seen when he visited – a thriving city or a hollowed-out ruin? And what impact did his visit have on both Troy itself and on how people understood the myth of the Trojan War?

Scene 2. An ageing scholar crouches over his desk, his quill poised over a clean piece of parchment. He must tell his tale from the beginning. Slowly, deliberately, he begins to write. The following words take shape on the page: 'After the Trojan War...'. The meticulous medieval monk was Geoffrey of Monmouth, the author of one of the earliest known works of British history, the *Historia Regum Britanniae* (History of the Kings of Britain). He began his history by introducing the first inhabitants of the island – the original Britons. These were, according to Geoffrey, Trojans fleeing the fall of Troy and enslavement by the Greeks. What was it, we might ask, that drew a twelfth-century Welsh cleric to locate the origins of Britain in Troy? Why did the myth of the Trojan War have such a strong hold over the medieval European imagination? And what significance did Geoffrey's claims have in a Britain riven by wars of dynastic succession, which was about to send crusaders on a route that passed the remains of Troy on their way to the Holy Land?

Scene 3. The steps of the town hall of Derry, Northern Ireland, in November 1995. On all sides there is the flashing of bulbs and the whirr of cameras. The speech is carried via loudspeakers to a crowd of 25,000 people packed into Guildhall Square. The speaker is heated and hopeful for the future. The time has come, he tells us, for the peacemakers to triumph. The time has come for hope and for history to rhyme. The speechmaker was Bill Clinton, quoting lines from Seamus Heaney's poem, *The Cure at Troy*, to mark the opening of a new chapter in the Northern Ireland peace process. But what led Clinton to quote a poem ostensibly dealing with a mythical ancient war in this particularly modern context? Why did the Derry-born Heaney address the internecine and sectarian conflict of his own time through the lens of a long-passed intercontinental siege? And what is it about the story of Troy that makes it still resonate with us today, nearly three millennia after it was first told?

н н н

Through the ages, Troy has meant many things to many people. This book attempts to trace the archaeological history of Troy by bringing together insights, not just from archaeology and history but also from literary and cultural studies, and research into reception.

The first section of the book focuses on the myth of Troy. In Chapter 2, we will explore this myth and its earliest known manifestations. As well as the many stories associated with the Trojan War, we will discuss the figure of Homer, the nature of epic poetry, and the particularities of the Greek epic tradition. Finally, we will consider the *Iliad* as a piece of literature and its particular portrayal of Troy. Chapter 3 tells a different, yet related, story – the story of discovery, excavation, and ongoing research at the archaeological site of Troy. This story of discovery has been shaped by the original myth of Troy, with successive generations of archaeologists measuring their work against the poetry of Homer. Chapter 4 considers how far we can match the myth with any sense of historical or archaeological truth. Did the Trojan War actually happen? What real-life historical events might the myth be based on?

The second section of the book turns from the myth to the city of Troy, and the periods of its occupation during antiquity. Starting with the Early Bronze Age in Chapter 5 and finishing with the Roman period in Chapter 10, this section charts the development of the city over time. Each chapter offers an overview of the archaeological remains of the site during the period in question, discussing the changing fortunes of Troy as a city and community between *c.* 3000 BCE and 700 CE. Alongside this primarily archaeological discussion, each chapter will explore contemporary representations of the Trojan War myth, and consider how the myth of Troy was understood in these different periods.

The final section of the book deals with the period from the seventh century CE onwards, when the city was no longer properly inhabited. As the site of Troy slipped into historical obscurity, the idea of Troy as an abstract cultural icon developed. The four chapters in this section are organized thematically, rather than chronologically. I have made no attempt to include a comprehensive overview of all instances where Troy has been referenced or the Trojan War story told, nor do I claim to cover all the ways in which Troy has been significant in the post-antique periods. Rather, these chapters aim to explore some of the key themes contributing to Troy's iconic status in the medieval, early modern, and modern worlds. These include the use of Troy in the construction of national origins and identities in Chapter 11, as a means of exploring love and desire in Chapter 12, and, in Chapter 13, as a lens through which to reflect on the nature of conflict in all its myriad forms. The story is brought up to date in Chapter 14, which considers Troy's place in the twentieth and twenty-first centuries as a symbol of both tragedy and hope. The idea of Troy today, as it has been in ages past, offers us a way of thinking through the human condition.

# The Making of a Myth

The story of Troy is inextricably linked with the tale of the Trojan War. In this chapter, we will explore this myth and how it was made. We will delve into the nature of epic poetry and the mysterious figure known as 'Homer', investigating how stories of the Trojan War were first composed and how they were circulated. We will then turn to the *Iliad* itself, considering the key themes of the poem and investigating how the city of Troy was portrayed in the epic. First, however, we must turn to the story at the heart of the matter – the myth of the Trojan War.

## The story of the Trojan War

The story of the Trojan War begins not with Troy, or even with the Achaean adversaries of Troy. Instead, the story begins in an idyllic setting on the high slopes of Mount Ida in the Troad. A young shepherd, Paris, is approached by three immortal goddesses: Hera, the queen of the gods; Athena, the goddess of wisdom; and Aphrodite, the goddess of love. The goddesses ask him to judge which of them is the most beautiful, awarding the winner a golden apple which had been specially inscribed 'for the most beautiful'. Paris bestows the apple on Aphrodite, who in return for this favour has promised him possession of the most beautiful woman in the world, Helen of Sparta. True to her word, when Paris is sent on a diplomatic mission to Sparta on behalf of his parents, King Priam and Queen Hecuba of Troy, Aphrodite arranges for him to meet the beautiful Helen and to carry her back with him to Troy. The stage for war was set.

Before Helen married her husband, Menelaus of Sparta, all of her many suitors had sworn an oath to defend her marriage. With Helen taken from him, Menelaus now called for the oath to be honoured, and gathered a huge army of these suitors and their troops. This motley army included many heroes, such as Achilles, Odysseus, Nestor, and Ajax, and was commanded by Menelaus' brother, Agamemnon of Mycenae. In early texts, the army is generally referred to as 'Achaean', rather than 'Greek' or 'Hellenic' (for a discussion of this, see Chapter 4). After some initial difficulties, the army set sail from Aulis in Boeotia. Arriving at Troy, the Achaeans camped on the beach at the edge of the plain of Troy and laid siege to the great city. The war was long and bloody, as the two sides were relatively evenly matched. The heroes of the Achaeans found themselves pitted against those of Troy and its allies, including Hector, Sarpedon, Penthesilea, and Memnon. Great feats of arms were accomplished on both sides, with the immortal gods often entering into the conflict to defend their particular favourites.

The deadlock was only broken in the tenth year of the war, when the god Apollo placed a curse on the Achaeans, blighting them with a terrible plague. When raiding in the surrounding countryside, the Achaeans had taken several women as war prizes, one of whom was Chryseis, the daughter of a priest of Apollo. When Agamemnon refused the generous ransom offered by Chryseis' father, the priest called on Apollo to curse the Achaeans with plague as vengeance. Agamemnon was forced to return the girl in order to lift the curse. As Achilles had spoken out against Agamemnon's treatment of the priest, Agamemnon sought to punish him by taking from him a different girl, Bryseis, who had originally been Achilles' war prize. Achilles was outraged at the insult, and withdrew from the war in anger. This falling out between the Achaeans' two most important leaders had major consequences for the course of the entire Trojan War.

With Achilles refusing to fight, the balance of the war tipped in favour of the Trojans, and the Achaeans suffered several heavy defeats. For some time, Achilles remained unmoved by the losses and ignored the entreaties of his comrades to return to combat. It was not until the death of his close friend Patroclus at the hands of Hector, the crown prince of Troy, that he took up arms again, this time motivated by a desire for revenge. Achilles' fury turned the tide of the war, and the Achaeans were able to put the Trojans to flight. Recognizing the nature of Achilles' wrath, Hector came to meet him in single combat, even though he knew it meant his own death. Achilles killed Hector in a dramatic duel beneath the walls of Troy, before mutilating his body and dragging the corpse back to his camp. Achilles only agreed to return Hector's body for burial after Hector's father, King Priam, approached him directly and offered him formal supplication. The death of Troy's greatest champion and the humbling of its king at the feet of Achilles marked another turning point in the war – after this moment, an Achaean victory became inevitable.

The Trojans sought the support of many allies in order to replace the leadership they had lost with Hector. These included the Amazons, whose queen, Penthesilea, was killed by Achilles, although not before he had fallen deeply in love with her. Memnon was another notable Trojan ally, the son of the goddess Dawn who led a detachment of Ethiopians into battle; he was also slain by Achilles. Not long afterwards, Achilles himself was killed by Paris, who shot him with an arrow in the only place where he was vulnerable – his heel. Paris was in turn killed by Philoctetes, an Achaean hero who carried the bow and arrows of Hercules. With so many significant figures dead on both sides, the Achaeans sought to end the war by deceit rather than by force of arms.

It is said that either Odysseus or the otherwise unknown figure of Epeius designed the wooden horse, within which a group of the Achaeans' best fighters were concealed. Seeing the Achaeans burning their huts and pretending to sail away, the Trojans rejoiced and, believing they had won the war, brought the horse into the city to celebrate their assumed victory. Only Cassandra, Troy's mad prophet, and the priest of Poseidon Laocoön argued against bringing the horse within the city walls. Their warnings, although unheeded, proved prescient. In the dark of night, the hidden soldiers slipped from the horse and opened the gates of the city for the Achaean army which had been waiting outside. In the sack of the city that followed, many of the Trojans were slaughtered and Troy was burnt to the ground.

Only a small group of Trojans escaped the sack of Troy, setting out under the leadership of Aeneas, a nephew of King Priam. These Trojan refugees eventually landed in Italy and founded Rome. The women of Troy who failed to escape, including Queen Hecuba and Andromache, the wife of Hector, were apportioned as war slaves to Achaean masters. As for the Achaeans, they set out for home a full decade after they had left, and the way home often proved harder than expected. Some, like Odysseus, had to undertake long and tortuous journeys; others, like Agamemnon, came home to find only strife and death; and yet others still, like the Achaean seer Calchas, never returned at all, but died along the way. The story of the Trojan War, it seems, had very few happy endings.

## Homer and epic poetry

We know the story of the Trojan War primarily through the Homeric epic, the *Iliad*. However, the *Iliad* only tells part of the story, focusing exclusively on the period between Apollo's plague on the Achaeans and the death of Hector. It is clear, however, that the poem expects its audience to be familiar with the wider tale, as allusions are made throughout the *Iliad* to episodes both before and after the actual narrative.

Around the time that the *Iliad* was composed in the eighth century BCE, the Trojan War was the subject of several different epic poems in Greek, known collectively as the Epic Cycle.[1] These poems are now mostly lost, but we are able to reconstruct their contents by piecing together the quotations and summaries contained in later texts.[2] The first of these poems following the chronological logic of the Trojan War is the *Cypria*, which sets the scene for the *Iliad* by recounting the judgement of Paris, the 'theft' of Helen from Sparta, the arrival of the Achaeans at Troy, and early skirmishes in the war. The *Iliad* would have come next in the series, beginning with the plague on the Achaeans and ending with the death of Hector. After this, the *Aethiopis* describes the deaths of several major heroes, in particular Penthesilea, Memnon, and Achilles. In the *Little Iliad*, we hear of the deaths of Ajax and Paris and the idea of the wooden horse, while the *Ilioupersis* is the tale of the actual sack of Troy. Following this, the *Nostoi* tells of how several Achaean heroes made the long journey home, while the *Odyssey* focuses on Odysseus' particularly difficult return. Finally, the *Telegony* recounts Odysseus' later adventures and his eventual death at the unwitting hands of his own son by the enchantress Circe, Telegonus.

The poems of the Epic Cycle, including the *Iliad*, emerged from a long-standing oral tradition. Anthropological studies have helped to highlight how such systems work. In oral traditions, stories are passed from person to person and generation to generation. During this process some tales would acquire a canonical form, usually in verse as the rhythm aids memorization. Other mnemonic devices such as repeated linking phrases, stock images, and standardized epithets are also common in oral traditions.[3] It is clear that the poems of the Greek Epic Cycle, and in particular Homeric poetry, feature many such mnemonic devices and that they originally developed out of an oral tradition.

This oral tradition is likely to have been very ancient indeed, and probably stretched back into the Late Bronze Age – one well-known fresco from the Mycenaean palace at Pylos depicts a bard singing to the accompaniment of a lyre (Figure 2.1). This tradition, although we now think of it as Greek, was most likely multilingual for several centuries between the Late Bronze and Early Iron Ages. Indeed, in early Greek epic we can find many motifs, patterns, and themes that are also to be found in epics from the Near East. Many features from the *Iliad*, for example, have parallels in the Mesopotamian epic of *Gilgamesh* – notably, the relationship between Achilles and Patroclus is comparable to that between the heroes Gilgamesh and Enkidu.[4] There is also evidence for a more immediate model for the Trojan War story in the poetry of Bronze Age Anatolia. One particular fragment of text found in the Hittite capital of Hattuša contains the

**Figure 2.1** Fresco from the Mycenaean palace at Pylos, showing a bard with a lyre.

opening of a choral song which begins: 'when they came from steep Wilusa...'. As will be discussed in more detail in Chapter 4, Wilusa was the name used amongst the Hittites for Troy, and this fragment therefore suggests that poetry about Troy was not only sung in Ancient Greek during the Iron Age, but also in Hurro-Hittite during the Late Bronze Age.[5]

The poems of the Epic Cycle, therefore, are most likely based on some very ancient material. However, these epics also seem to have undergone a deliberate process of composition at a particular point in time. This composition involved not only the reworking of traditional poetic features from the oral tradition but also the introduction of original elements. Composition may also have involved the use of the new technology of writing in the Greek script, although it is unclear what role writing may have had in the formation of early Greek epic.[6] This combination of the oral and the literate, the traditional and the innovative, has led to speculation about the identity of the poet known as Homer, including whether Homer was an individual or a group of poets.[7] In any case, the Homeric epics seem to have been composed somewhere in the eastern Aegean or western

Anatolia, as their language is most closely related to the local dialects of this area. This likely happened at some stage during the eighth century, with the *Odyssey* composed some time after the *Iliad*. Other poems in the Epic Cycle may have been composed as late as the sixth century BCE.[8]

Epic poetry was not the only way that stories about the Trojan War would have been told. Traditional tales such as these would have circulated in many different forms and through many different media, in much the same way that common fairy tales are circulated today. The Trojan War story was also depicted in the visual arts, and in particular in decorated pottery.[9] Although it is not until the seventh century that we can identify a Trojan War scene on pottery with certainty (Figure 2.2),[10] it seems likely that some earlier images of warfare and combat may also have represented episodes from the Trojan War. In addition, informal representations of the stories would also have abounded, from the simplified versions that parents might tell children to oblique references, jokes, and puns in everyday discussion. By its nature, this informal tradition surrounding the Trojan War would have been flexible and ephemeral, and unlikely to have survived in our existing source material.[11] It would, nonetheless, have been an important part of the wider context within which the *Iliad* was heard and interpreted, and we should therefore bear it in mind.

In order to understand the *Iliad* fully, therefore, we must recognize that it was part of a wider set of traditions surrounding the Trojan War story – both the formal traditions that gave rise to the Epic Cycle and works of visual art and the informal traditions that may have included common jokes, proverbs, and everyday conversation.

## Troy and the *Iliad*

As we have already noted, the *Iliad* does not tell the entire story of the Trojan War, but instead focuses on a period of about forty days midway through the tenth year of the siege. It is obvious from this that the central theme of the poem is not the Trojan War *per se*. Rather, the *Iliad* is about something rather more complex – conflict and reconciliation, in many different forms and at many different levels.[12]

The poem signals this from its very first line, instructing the muse to sing the rage of Achilles (*menin aeide thea…*; Goddess, sing the rage…). 'Rage' is the first word of the epic, and the poem goes on to explore both the workings and

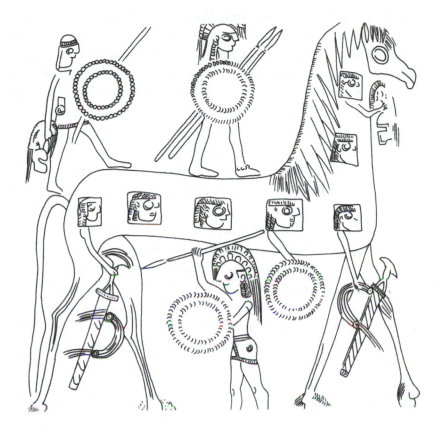

**Figure 2.2** Neck of a Cycladic relief vase found on Mykonos depicting the Trojan Horse, *c.* 675–650 BCE.

the consequences of this rage for both the individual and the community. At one level, it focuses on the internal conflict raging within Achilles about honour and mortality. This internal conflict is particularly well explored in a conversation between Achilles and his mother Thetis on the beach after the quarrel with Agamemnon.[13] It is finally resolved in a later conversation between the two after the death of Patroclus, with Achilles resigning himself to the inevitability of fate and accepting the futility of his own rage in the face of necessity (*ananke*).[14] Conflict and reconciliation within the psyche of an individual are therefore a key theme of the poem.

The *Iliad* also explores conflict at several other levels – between the individual and society, within a community, and between communities. In each case, the figure of Achilles is used to explore this conflict. The conflict between the individual and society is manifested in Achilles' self-imposed isolation following his dispute with Agamemnon. His rejection of social relationships is made particularly obvious in Book 9, when he rebuffs the entreaties of Odysseus which are made on the basis of duty, those of his tutor Phoenix which are made on the basis of family ties, and those of Ajax which are made on the basis of friendship.[15] One by one, Achilles rejects the different social bonds that should hold him. It is not until Book 24, when Achilles accepts the supplication of Priam and returns the body of his dead son Hector, that Achilles reintegrates into society. He recognizes that he has transgressed the ultimate moral law by mistreating a corpse and is moved, not by the pleas of his friends and comrades, but by those of his Trojan enemy. The universality of human social relations is restored.

The poem also reflects on conflict at the level of the community, focusing on how different systems of value and status lead to friction amongst members of a community. This is perhaps most evident in the argument between Achilles and Agamemnon in Book 1, which is only fully resolved when Agamemnon helps Achilles to bury Patroclus in Book 23. While Achilles is described as 'best' (*aristos*) of the Achaeans for his strength and martial prowess, Agamemnon is the 'most kingly' (*basileutatos*) for his authority and high standing. The disjoint between these two competing systems of value – acquired and ascribed status – leads to conflict within the community of the Achaeans. This intra-communal conflict represents a shift from a social system based on individual prowess to one based on laws and government. At the time that the *Iliad* was composed in the eighth century BCE, Greek communities were coming together into city states, or *poleis* (singular: *polis*). An old system based on warrior pre-eminence was declining, and in its place was emerging a new system based on citizenship, laws, and formal codes of authority.

On a more obvious level, the *Iliad* also deals with conflict between communities, and this is evident in its portrayal of the war as a whole. This conflict between communities is evident not only in the bloody descriptions of fighting and dying, which occur throughout the poem, but also in the detailed description of the two cities on Achilles' shield – the city in peace and the city at war.[16]

The depiction of the two cities on Achilles' shield mirrors Homer's own portrayal of Troy. Although the figure of Achilles may seem to be the central character in the narrative, it is the city of Troy that lies at the true heart of the story. After all, the epic itself is named for the city, as Troy was also known by a second name in antiquity – Ilion. The *Iliad* is, therefore, the story of Ilion.[17] Throughout the poem, Troy is represented as an ideal, or perhaps idealized, city.

The urban centre is described as a strong and a holy (*hieros*) citadel, surrounded by impregnable walls and high towers, within which are palaces and temples.[18] Notably, the epithets used to describe Troy are overwhelmingly concerned with how physically imposing it is – these include 'well-built' (*eudmetos*), 'well-walled' (*euteichos*), 'well-towered' (*eupyrgos*), and 'the great city' (*asty mega*).[19]

Troy is also used to depict the ideals of society and community, as well as the ideals of urban physicality. This is illustrated in Book 6, in which most of the action takes place within the city itself. The Trojans are on the back foot in the fighting, and Helenus, one of Priam's sons, reminds them about the importance of giving due honour to the gods and suggests that Hector return to the city to arrange sacrifices to Athena. This is followed by an encounter between the Trojan ally, Glaucus, and the Achaean Diomedes, who part cordially after they realize that their families are linked by guest-friendship (*xenia*).[20] Upon entering the city, Hector goes into the royal palace and meets first his mother, Hecuba, engaging her in a conversation about duty and the gods. He then comes upon the Trojan women at the temple of Athena, before meeting his brother Paris and upbraiding him for not fulfilling his martial duty. He then finds his wife Andromache at the city wall, and the two engage in a fond exchange discussing family love, romantic attachment, and civic duty.[21] Within Book 6, therefore, we are treated to a series of poignant reflections on the social ties that bind an individual: to their city and community, to their family and loved ones, to friends from other families and countries, and to the gods. While the camp of the Achaeans is depicted as a dysfunctional society (riven by internal conflict, and a place where individuals reject social bonds), the city of Troy is represented as its opposite – an ideal *polis*.

As already mentioned, the concept of the *polis* was beginning to emerge in the eighth century BCE at the time the *Iliad* was composed. The *polis* was both a physical and a social entity – on the one hand, it comprised the city and its territory, and on the other it consisted of the community of citizens. The Troy of the *Iliad* embodies these two central ideals.

# The Story of Discovery

The myth of Troy echoed through the centuries, inspiring many intrepid adventurers to seek out the remains of the lost city. A fierce debate raged in the eighteenth and nineteenth centuries over its location, with explorers and antiquarians championing different sites. It was not until the very end of the nineteenth century that a consensus emerged, and the location of Troy was agreed. With its cast of eccentric heroes and tragic victims, dastardly villains and dramatic twists of fate, the story of the discovery of Troy is itself a tale of epic proportions.

## The lost city

For centuries, the whereabouts of the ancient city of Troy were unknown. During the medieval and early modern periods, travellers and explorers proposed several sites in the Troad as the possible location, using ancient texts as guides (Map 2). One of the likely sites was that of Alexandria Troas, as it had impressive ruins which were clearly visible above ground. Another candidate was the site of Sigeon or Yenişehir, where the remains of a city wall from late antiquity could still be seen. Yet, neither site had a clear claim to being Troy, and some disappointed visitors to the Troad doubted that the lost city could ever be found. In 1718, for example, the British poet Mary Wortley Montagu sadly wrote: 'all that is now left of Troy is the ground on which it stood'.[1]

It was not until the Comte de Choiseul-Gouffier was appointed as the French Ambassador to the Ottoman Empire in 1784 that a serious attempt was made to identify the site of the lost city. The Comte sponsored a detailed survey of the entire Troad, leading to the discovery of two important new sites, both of which seemed to be likely candidates for the location of Troy: Pınarbaşı and Hisarlık. Although little in the way of impressive ruins remained at these sites, their locations in relation to key features such as rivers and mountains seemed to fit the geographical descriptions found in Homer.

Over the next century, a series of philologists, geologists, engineers, diplomats, and gentleman-explorers championed one or the other of these two sites in an increasingly heated debate. One eighteenth-century visitor reviewed a book arguing in favour of Pınarbaşı as: 'speculation … no more than the gay dream of a Classical enthusiast'. In the early nineteenth century, the British poet Byron snidely remarked that the Troad was 'a fine field for conjecture and snipe-shooting'.[2]

It was not until the mid-nineteenth century that a strong case for Hisarlık was put forward. Frank Calvert, a British expatriate living in the Ottoman Empire, had undertaken extensive explorations in the Troad, and was convinced that the mound of Hisarlık concealed the ancient city of Troy. Calvert was so confident of his identification that he purchased as much of the land around Hisarlık as he could, intending to excavate the mound himself. Calvert's early excavations yielded promising results, but a lack of resources prevented him from pursuing them further.[3] Calvert needed a wealthy patron to advance his work. But the man he eventually won over to his cause – Heinrich Schliemann – proved to be a far cry from the sponsor and silent partner that Calvert had hoped for.

## Schliemann: The Homeric quest

When Heinrich Schliemann visited him on his tour of the Troad in 1868, Calvert thought he had found the ideal collaborator. Schliemann was wealthy, having made his fortune in commodities trading, and enthusiastic, gripped by a romantic vision of discovering the lost city of Priam and Hector.[4] Under their original agreement, Calvert was to contribute his archaeological expertise and allow Schliemann access to his land, while Schliemann would underwrite the costs of the excavation. As things turned out, Schliemann had little time for Calvert's advice and expertise, preferring to follow his instincts and pursue his own private vision. The relationship between Schliemann and Calvert was fraught, and although recent research has vindicated Calvert's interpretations over those of Schliemann, posterity remembers the colourful Schliemann far more readily than it does the hardworking Calvert.[5]

Schliemann must have cut something of a strange figure, feverishly directing his workers on the site of Hisarlık. He was by all accounts rather socially awkward, portly in stature, and pompous in bearing, with a deep sense of self-belief and a righteous indignation against all those who disagreed with him (Figure 3.1).

**Figure 3.1** Photograph of Heinrich Schliemann.

Schliemann also had a chequered past. He had made his fortune in business –
first in the Crimea and later in the Californian Gold Rush – not always, it seems,
by strictly legal means. In 1868, at the age of forty-six, his wealth was such that
he was able to retire from business and devote himself to his private passion –
Homeric archaeology. He visited the Troad, meeting Frank Calvert and striking
a deal to excavate Hisarlık, in that very same year. Schliemann's Homeric quest
had begun.

Over the next twenty-two years, Schliemann was to excavate first at the site of Troy and later at Mycenae and Tiryns on the Greek mainland, making spectacular finds. His contributions to archaeology are considerable. It was Schliemann who first uncovered the societies of the Late Bronze Age Aegean – what is now known as the 'Mycenaean world' – and demonstrated that these societies were complex and interesting in their own right, not merely as the barbaric precursors to classical Greece. It was Schliemann who first identified the Late Bronze Age as the original setting for the myths of the Greek Epic Cycle – the 'heroic age' encoded in the cultural memory of later Greeks. Finally, and most importantly for the purposes of this book, it was Schliemann who firmly established that the site of Hisarlık was to be equated with the ancient settlement of Troy or Ilion.[6] This final achievement is all the more impressive for being accomplished at a time when most professional scholars, and particularly classicists, did not believe that Troy was a historical place or that there was any historical basis for the myth of the Trojan War.[7]

Schliemann's contributions to scholarship must, however, be considered alongside the many problems with his work. First, the quality of his work was poor and methods were outdated even by the standards of the time. He excavated speedily and in great volume, destroying large amounts of the archaeological record and failing to document much of what was uncovered along the way. This was not helped by the fact that, until relatively late in his life, he bullishly ignored the advice of friends and critics which would have helped him improve his archaeological methods. Calvert was only one of the many that he treated in this way.

Second, Schliemann's integrity was highly questionable. He flaunted both official regulations and private agreements: stealing finds from sites for his own private collection; denying government representatives access to his finds; excavating without permits; and cheating his collaborators and colleagues. He also frequently lied in his published work about the nature of his excavations and discoveries. This mendacity seems to have been a common feature of his personal life and business arrangements as well as his archaeological work.[8]

This archaeological work was driven by a deep personal passion for the classical past, bordering on obsession. His diaries document his attempts to lead his own life in a Homeric fashion and record at every turn his tendency to project visions of antiquity into the present day. When he divorced his first wife, he was determined to 'marry a girl of pure Greek heritage who resembled Helen of Troy … she should be unsophisticated as well as good-looking… [like a] docile and obedient plant, clever and intelligent.' The girl he eventually did settle on was the seventeen-year-old Sophia Engastromenos. He was forty-seven at the time. With his very own Helen at his side and a copy of the *Iliad* in his hand, Schliemann embarked on his excavations of Hisarlık, desperate to prove the historical accuracy of the epic. His almost-religious belief in Homer lay behind both his greatest discoveries and his greatest failures.

The most famous and scandalous of these was the 'Treasure of Priam'.[9] Towards the end of this third season of excavation at Troy in 1873, Schliemann claimed to have uncovered a spectacular cache of gold, silver, and copper artefacts (Figure 3.2). The hoard included metal vessels, weapons, silver weights, and an impressive quantity of jewellery. Schliemann was quick to dub the find the 'Treasure of Priam', and to suggest that it had been packed up hastily by some member of the Trojan royal family fleeing the sack of the city. His published accounts of its discovery attracted widespread public interest and caused something of a sensation in the archaeological world. Indeed, his description of finding the treasure reads like an extract from an adventure novel: a priceless ancient treasure is uncovered by an intrepid adventurer, who risks his life to save it from theft and confiscation.

> In excavating this wall further and directly by the side of the palace of King Priam, I came upon a large copper article of the most remarkable form, which attracted my attention all the more as I thought I saw gold behind it... In order to withdraw the Treasure from the greed of my workmen, and to save it for archaeology, I had to be most expeditious, and although it was not yet time for breakfast, I immediately had '*paidos*' called ... While the men were eating and resting, I cut out the Treasure with a large knife, which it was impossible to do without the very greatest exertion and the most fearful risk of my life, for the great fortification-wall, beneath which I had to dig, threatened every moment to fall down upon me. But the sight of so many objects, every one of which is of inestimable value to archaeology, made me foolhardy, and I never thought of any danger. It would, however, have been impossible for me to have removed the Treasure without the help of my dear wife, who stood ready to pack the things which I cut out in her shawl and to carry them away.
>
> Schliemann 1875, 323–4

This discovery, Schliemann argued, was the proof that the site of Hisarlık had been a wealthy and important city in the time of the Homeric heroes – a city that could only have been the Troy of the *Iliad*. His writings on the subject of the Treasure inspired as much criticism as praise, however, and major inconsistencies soon emerged. It quickly became evident that Schliemann had lied about the circumstances of the Treasure's discovery and excavation, as well as its findspot, and even its identification as a coherent hoard. The objects had

**Figure 3.2** The 'Treasure of Priam'.

in fact been uncovered at different points during the excavation and had been assembled into a single 'treasure' by Schliemann himself. The very discovery that Schliemann hoped would prove his argument had instead tainted his entire enterprise with scandal.

Today, our approach to the Treasure is similar to our understanding of Schliemann's discoveries more generally. While the objects themselves are acknowledged as being archaeologically significant, we no longer accept either the context or the interpretation for them suggested by their excavator. Crucially, we now know that the artefacts comprising the Treasure do not date to the Late Bronze Age, the time during which a supposed Trojan War is thought to have happened, but rather to the Early Bronze Age, some 800 or so years before.

## Dörpfeld: The nine cities of Troy

Towards the end of his life, Schliemann employed the young architect and archaeologist Wilhelm Dörpfeld to help him, both at Troy and at the site of Tiryns. Dörpfeld was responsible for introducing a more rigorous stratigraphic method to the excavations, and was able to distinguish nine distinct settlement levels at Hisarlık. He labelled these Troy I–IX, from the oldest to the most recent (Map 3). The stratigraphic sequence established by Dörpfeld continues to form the basis for our understanding of the site today.

The layering of different settlement levels over each other is a characteristic feature of many Anatolian and Near Eastern sites. Since the walls of buildings were usually made from mudbricks resting on stone foundations, these would collapse in onto each other whenever the settlement was destroyed or a building was damaged. Such destructions could have a range of different causes, including the inhabitants choosing to flatten an area to make way for a new construction project, domestic accidents such as house fires, attackers violently burning the settlement, and natural disasters such as earthquakes. After a destruction horizon, the remnants of the old buildings would be levelled off and compacted down to create a suitable surface for new buildings. The new occupation level would therefore be built on top of the old. Even at times when there were no dramatic destruction events, the continual repair of buildings and the everyday accumulation of debris and rubbish would mean that, periodically, the settlement would need clearing and structures would need to be renewed. Inevitably, over many centuries the height of this surface would rise, and the settlement would come to resemble a mound. Such mounds are known as *tells* (in Arabic) or *höyüks* (in Turkish), and often consist of many metres of settlement stratigraphy resting on a natural hill or escarpment.

Dörpfeld continued to excavate at Troy after Schliemann's death in 1890 for a further two years and succeeded in learning much more about the nature of the site. As well as the nine major settlement levels, he also identified a series of architectural subphases within these levels. He realized that the top of the mound had been shaved off in antiquity, levelled during the Hellenistic period to create an artificially flat surface on which the monumental Temple of Athena was built. This meant that the prehistoric levels had been much closer to the surface than anyone had realized.

It became evident that Schliemann, in his eagerness to reach what he thought would be the Homeric level, had actually dug through and discarded most of the prehistoric remains at the centre of the mound. Through careful study, Dörpfeld was able to reassign Troy II, which Schliemann had thought represented Homeric Troy, to the Early Bronze Age. He also identified Troy VI as the main Late Bronze Age level, and recognized that it had eight subphases which he labelled a–h. Most of these subphases were not the result of destruction horizons, but had been produced by the regular remodelling of the settlement by its own inhabitants.

The latest of these subphases, Troy VIh, was a large and impressive city with imposing stone fortifications enclosing several large houses, some of which contained rich finds including imports from Mesopotamia, Egypt, and Cyprus. Unlike many previous phases, Troy VIh did seem to have been levelled in a major destruction horizon, involving a fierce blaze that raged across the settlement. This, Dörpfeld argued, must have been the city of the Trojan War, razed to the ground by the Homeric Achaeans.[10]

## Blegen: Analysis and refinement

After Dörpfeld left Hisarlık in 1894, it was not until 1932 that the site was excavated again, this time by Carl Blegen and the University of Cincinnati. Blegen introduced new archaeological methods to the site, including more precise approaches to stratigraphy and ceramic dating. In particular, a systematic study of the finds allowed Blegen to assess the extent of cultural change and continuity. For the first time, close attention was paid to all levels of the mound, not only the level deemed to be Homeric.[11] Blegen's main focus, however, remained the prehistoric phases, and he made significant revisions to Dörpfeld's interpretation of Homeric Troy.

In particular, Blegen noted that there was considerable cultural continuity not only across all the subphases of Troy VI, but also in the first subphase of Troy VII. The ceramics, artefacts, and even the layout and buildings of Troy VIIa all looked conspicuously similar to those of the preceding Troy VIh phase, leading Blegen to suggest that the same population continued to occupy the site. He argued that the fiery destruction which ended Troy VIh was not the handiwork of hostile invaders, but was more likely due to an earthquake. This would explain why the inhabitants remained the same, and why Troy VIIa looked like a hastily rebuilt version of Troy VIh. According to Blegen therefore, it was not Troy VIh that was the Homeric city, but rather Troy VIIa.

This later phase also showed evidence of being ravaged by a fire, but this time arrowheads and unburied skeletons were discovered in the ashy debris, implying that the destruction had been violent. In addition, Blegen pointed out that when the large, grand buildings of Troy VIh were rebuilt in Troy VIIa, they were often subdivided with party walls, suggesting that many more people had moved into the citadel by the end of this phase. This, Blegen argued, was a likely sign of a city under siege, as the people occupying the surrounding areas and the plain would have crowded into the fortified city to escape the invaders.[12]

Blegen published the results of his work in a methodical and scientific way, making the data from the Troy excavations available for scholars and interested readers everywhere. This allowed for further crucial analysis of the finds and comparison between sites. Troy quickly became a 'type-site' for western Anatolia, setting the standard against which other sites were measured.

## Korfmann and Rose: Total Troy

The third series of excavations at Troy began in 1988, with Manfred Korfmann directing the Bronze Age research, and Brian Rose directing work on the post-Bronze Age remains. For the first time, equal attention was paid to both the prehistoric and historic levels, and a holistic view over the site's history was developed.[13]

The latest scientific techniques were applied to the site, including radiocarbon dating to establish a firmer chronology; thin section and neutron activation analysis to identify the composition and origin of ceramics; provenancing analysis for metal and stone artefacts to ascertain their place and means of manufacture; zooarchaeology and archaeobotany to shed light on farming practices and food supplies; and geoarchaeology and sediment studies to determine the nature of the ancient climate and environment.

One of the major discoveries resulting from this work was that of the lower city on the plain beneath Hisarlık. Using a combination of geophysical survey and targeted excavations, the team was able to establish that there had once been an extensive settlement at the foot of the mound, covering some 200,000–300,000 square metres at is maximum extent.[14] It now seems, therefore, that for much of its history the mound of Hisarlık was only a small part of a much larger settlement. It would have been a fortified citadel where important administrative buildings were located, while the majority of the population lived in the sprawling settlement on the plain. This discovery had significant implications for our understanding of the size and importance of Troy.

Other important advances made by the Korfmann–Rose team included the discovery of a system of underground water channels carved into the bedrock dating back to the Early Bronze Age, and several surveys of the surrounding area and the Troad which served to put the findings at Troy into their wider regional context.

Although the work of the Korfmann–Rose team did not officially focus on Homeric Troy, Korfmann inevitably became involved in discussions of the Trojan War. Korfmann largely agreed with Blegen's conclusions about Troy VIIa, arguing that the lower city displayed similar signs of deliberate and violent destruction to those that had been found on the citadel. Not only was the lower city thoroughly burned, but weaponry and ammunition were discovered in the ashes, as well as unburied bodies. In addition, he argued that the existence of the lower city was itself also testament to the wealth and significance of Troy at the end of the Late Bronze Age, making it a city worthy of Homeric epic. Although Korfmann tended to avoid making firm claims about the Trojan War in his academic writings, when pressed on the historicity of the war during an interview for a popular magazine, his response was 'why not?'[15]

From 2001 onwards, a fierce and often bitter debate raged about Korfmann's findings at Troy. One of Korfmann's colleagues at the University of Tübingen, Frank Kolb, attacked Korfmann's interpretation of the site as being deliberately misleading. The debate was carried out not only in the pages of academic books and journals but also in the popular press.[16] It is interesting that many of the themes of this recent debate were the same as those featuring in the controversy surrounding Schliemann: the size of the settlement, its wealth, the correct application of new archaeological methods, and the personal integrity of site director. In contrast with Schliemann, however, scholarly opinion now weighs in favour of Korfmann, and while many might not agree with his broadly historicist perspective on the Trojan War, few would doubt the veracity of his finds or the robustness of his general conclusions.

After Korfmann's death in 2005, work continued at the site until 2012 under the direction of Rose and Korfmann's deputies, Peter Jablonka and Ernst Pernicka. Since then, there has been discussion of renewed research at Hisarlık, perhaps conducted by a joint Turkish-American team. Indeed, there remain many potentially fruitful areas for future archaeological investigation. Substantial areas of the mound remain, mostly around the outer edges which were untouched by Schliemann, and only a small proportion of the lower city has thus far been explored. In addition, the dump where Schliemann deposited the soil excavated from the centre of the mound has yet to be investigated, and this is likely to be rich in remains from the Late Bronze Age. The story of Trojan discovery is far from over.

# 4

# The Truth about the Trojan War

Most scholars would now agree that the archaeological site known as Troy – the mound of Hisarlık and its immediate environs – are the remains of the city known in antiquity as Ilion or Troy. In the classical world, all cities had their own myths and legends, and every town had stories that its inhabitants told about their glorious past and ancestral heroes. The city of Troy had perhaps the best-known and most spectacular of all these civic myths – the story of the Trojan War.

But is there any historical basis for many legends of Troy? Is it possible to bring together the myths we explored in Chapter 2 with the archaeology we discussed in Chapter 3? What is the truth about the Trojan War?

## The real Trojans

There can be no doubt that the area around Hisarlık was known in classical antiquity as Troy or Ilion. Numerous inscriptions have been found from the Hellenistic and Roman periods that explicitly name the settlement as Ilion.[1] In addition, the city began to mint its own coins from the end of the fourth century BCE onwards, bearing the inscription in Greek letters: IΛI (or 'ILI', short for 'Ilion').[2] As we shall find in Chapters 9 and 10, Ilion in the Hellenistic and Roman periods was a populous and prosperous city, attracting many visitors to the monumental temple of Athena, which stood on the summit of the citadel mound.

It is less obvious whether Hisarlık had always been known as Ilion, as no written records have been found at the site which bears witness to the city's name in prehistory. Some helpful written sources exist from the Late Bronze Age, belonging not to the Greco-Roman literary tradition (which begins in the eighth century BCE with Homer) but rather to the archives of the Hittite Empire (which mostly date to the fifteenth–thirteenth centuries BCE). The Hittites controlled a substantial empire in the Late Bronze Age, which was based at Hattuša on the central Anatolian plateau, and at its peak stretched from western Anatolia to northern Syria.

The imperial archives record, amongst other things, Hittite interactions with the states on the western fringe of the empire in western Anatolia and the Aegean. This patchwork of small, independent principalities had a complex relationship with the Hittites, sometimes aligning themselves with Hattuša and at other times engaging the Hittites in open conflict. Several Hittite kings attempted to quell the troublesome region and to bring it under the imperial yoke, but they were unable to control western Anatolia for long and any Hittite influence has left relatively little trace in the archaeological record.[3]

One of these western Anatolian states was the kingdom of Wilusa, the name of which is etymologically linked to the Greek word 'Ilion'.[4] While it has long been suggested that Wilusa and Ilion may be the same place, firm evidence to support this theory only emerged in the 1990s. In particular, new inscriptions have been deciphered which gave us a clearer sense of Hittite geography, locating Wilusa firmly in northwestern Anatolia.[5] In one particular text, a place known as Taruisa is also mentioned in relation to Wilusa, and it has been suggested that Taruisa was the Hittite name for the citadel of Troy, while Wilusa was used to refer to the Troad as a whole.[6] Whatever the location of Taruisa however, we can nonetheless be confident that Ilion or Troy was a real place, and that it was known as Wilusa in the Late Bronze Age. We will return to the history of Late Bronze Age Troy in Chapter 6.


## The real 'Greeks'

In the Greek Epic Cycle, the army that fought against Troy is referred to in several different ways. Collectively, they are most commonly called Achaeans, but they are sometimes also known as Danaans, or Argives. Significantly, they are never referred to as Hellenes, and certainly not as 'Greeks'. This last term was developed relatively late in antiquity and comes from the Latin name for the Greeks (Graeci). It was therefore not a term that the Ancient Greeks used when referring to themselves. It is clear that the idea of a Greek collective identity had not yet emerged at the time that Homer wrote, as the later Greek author Thucydides acknowledged (Thucydides, *History of the Peloponnesian War* 1.2). When we say today that the Trojan War was fought between the 'Greeks' and the

Trojans, we are casting the war in nationalistic terms which would have been wholly unfamiliar to Homer's original audience.

In this book, I shall use terms that are appropriate to the context under discussion. We will therefore talk about 'Achaeans' when discussing the besiegers of Troy in the original myths of the Trojan War, but will refer to these same characters as 'Greeks' in the context of later representations and reinterpretations of the story.

But who were the Achaeans, the Danaans, and the Argives? These three groups can be securely located on the southern Greek mainland: in classical times, Achaea was a region in the northern Peloponnese; while the Argolid was located in the northeastern Peloponnese. The term 'Danaans' also relates to people from Argos, referring to them as the descendants of Danaus, the mythical prince of Egypt who settled with his fifty daughters at Argos. When the units comprising the Achaean army are listed in the *Iliad* however, it is evident that not all of them hailed from either Achaea or Argos.[7] The locations cited in this list are all familiar place names from the classical period in southern and central Greece, with some on Crete and some of the east and west Aegean islands (although none from the Cyclades).

How can we explain this disjoint between the wide geographical spread of the allies, and the narrow geographical area implied by the collective terms 'Achaeans' and 'Argives'? There are two possible explanations. First, the geographical connotations of 'Achaea' and 'Argos' may have changed over time; when Homer wrote in the eighth century, the terms may have had a much wider meaning than they came to have in the classical period. It is also possible that the army as a whole was referred to by the region of its commander in chief – Agamemnon's hometown of Mycenae was located on the border of Achaea and Argolis.

In any case, it is evident that the homelands of the Achaeans, as described in the Homeric epics, were real historical locations. Not only are these locations known from the classical and later periods, but many were also occupied during the Late Bronze Age. These include: Mycenae, the seat of Agamemnon; Sparta, the home of Menelaus and Helen; Pylos and the palace of Nestor; and Salamis, the realm of Ajax. What is known as 'Mycenaean' culture flourished in these and other places in the Aegean, and grand palaces have been uncovered at both Mycenae and Pylos. Just as Troy seems to have been a real city, so too were the homes of Troy's foes. But if the locations mentioned in the Trojan War myth are historical, does it necessarily mean that the events and characters of the story are factual too?

## The real wars at Troy

As we saw in Chapter 2, the poems of the Greek Epic Cycle grew out of an ancient oral tradition which stretched back centuries before the poems' composition. It has been argued that such stories may have their origins in real historical events. Accounts of such events could have been preserved in the oral tradition, told from generation to generation.[8] In this way, stories about real events that happened in the Late Bronze or Early Iron Ages may have survived four or five centuries into the eighth century BCE. It is possible that this may have happened in the case of the Trojan War.

There is evidence in the archaeological record for not one but several wars at the site of Troy in the Late Bronze and Early Iron Ages. At three separate points, the city was burned and destroyed.

1. Troy VIh (destroyed *c.* 1300 BCE): In Chapter 3, we saw how Wilhelm Dörpfeld, one of Troy's excavators, interpreted the burnt destruction layer at the end of Troy VIh as the Achaean sack of the city. As we will discuss in more detail in Chapter 6, the same evidence is now interpreted as being caused by a natural disaster, most likely an earthquake.
2. Troy VIIa (destroyed *c.* 1180 BCE): The violent destruction that ended the Troy VIIa phase does seem to have been caused by a hostile armed attack, as we shall see at the end of Chapter 6. Carl Blegen, another one of Troy's excavators, argued that this layer marked the end of the Trojan War. The city in this period, however, was not as grand or impressive as we might expect from Homer's descriptions. In addition, the Mycenaean palaces had been destroyed before Troy VIIa, making it unlikely that the kings of southern and central Greece were responsible for this particular sack of Troy.
3. Troy VIIb$_2$ (destroyed *c.* 1050 BCE): This phase seems to have ended with the settlement being destroyed and temporarily abandoned, although the surviving archaeological evidence is scanty, as we shall see in Chapter 7. It is possible that the cause was a natural disaster rather than violence. As with Troy VIIa, the poverty of the city during this period does not match Homer's descriptions of Troy. And as with Troy VIIa, this destruction postdates the fall of the Mycenaean kingdoms and so is highly unlikely to have been caused by Aegean powers.

While the archaeology of Troy therefore gives us three potential candidates for a 'real' Trojan War, none is an obvious match for the Homeric conflict. But archaeology is not the only record of the real wars fought at Troy. The documents of the Hittite archives also make reference to at least four conflicts in and around Late Bronze Age Wilusa.

1. In the late fifteenth century BCE, Wilusa entered into an alliance of western Anatolian states against the Hittites known as the Assuwa Confederacy. According to Hittite records, the Confederacy was quickly crushed.[9]
2. Later, in the early thirteenth century BCE, we hear of Wilusa being attacked by an unnamed enemy and requiring Hittite assistance.[10]
3. Again in the thirteenth century, the records mention Wilusa being defeated by the Hittites, who imposed a new alliance and peace treaty on the city.[11]
4. Finally, in the late thirteenth century, we hear about civil strife in Wilusa and dynastic rivalries, which the local ruler called upon the Hittites to resolve.[12]

These four wars are unlikely to be the only ones that Wilusa was involved in during the Late Bronze Age. The existing sources record the history of Wilusa from a Hittite perspective, and so only mention conflicts in which the Hittites had some involvement or interest. They are also likely to exaggerate Hittite power and influence. If documents written by the Wilusians themselves had survived, we might have heard a very different story. In any case, the texts establish that there were several different wars fought at Wilusa in the Late Bronze Age, and at least three in the turbulent thirteenth century.

It is unclear if any of these historically attested conflicts can be identified with the Homeric Trojan War. The first does feature a coalition of western Anatolian powers in much the way that the *Iliad* describes Troy's allies. However, the enemy here is not Achaeans from the western Aegean but rather Hittites from the east. In addition, there is some evidence that some Mycenaean states were actually a part of the coalition against the Hittites, fighting on the same side as the Wilusans rather than against them.[13] The second conflict also does not match the story of the Trojan War, as although the unnamed aggressor against Wilusa may indeed have been an Aegean-based coalition from the west, it appears that in this case Wilusa was the victor. The third and fourth wars similarly do not fit the Homeric bill, as the one was fought against the Hittites and the other involved internal infighting and political factions within Wilusa.

It is evident that Troy during the Late Bronze and Early Iron Ages was a city that saw regular conflicts, that made and broke alliances, and that enjoyed victories as well as suffering defeats. It is certainly imaginable, therefore, that the story of the Trojan War has at its heart the memory of a real historical conflict. However, none of the known conflicts of the Late Bronze and Early Iron Ages correspond to the myth of the Trojan War. We have no evidence of any real war in which Troy/Wilusa was besieged and defeated by the Mycenaean states of the western Aegean. So while we have proof of many wars at Troy, we have no evidence yet for the Trojan War itself.

## The wars of Troy in context

We know, then, that Troy was involved in several wars during the Late Bronze and Early Iron Ages. We also know that Troy was not unique in this respect. Most other states in the Aegean and Anatolia experienced similar levels of fighting. The city of Miletus, located to the south of Troy on the Aegean coast of Anatolia, provides a good illustration of this.

The archaeological evidence shows that Miletus was destroyed three times during the Late Bronze Age, at least once at the hands of enemy attackers.[14] We hear of yet more conflicts at Miletus in the Hittite sources, if we follow the general consensus that the Hittite name for Miletus was Millawanda or Milawata. The city was sacked by the Hittites following its involvement in an anti-Hittite coalition during the fourteenth century; used as a base for raids in the surrounding region the warlord Piyamaradu in the mid-thirteenth century; and subdued by the Hittite king and his local western Anatolian allies in the late thirteenth century.[15] The commonness of conflict in the nearby Aegean is also illustrated by the destruction of the Minoan palaces midway through the Late Bronze Age, and of the Mycenaean palaces towards the end of the Bronze Age. The history of both the Aegean and Anatolia during this time is characterized by wars, sieges, and alliances.

Perhaps unsurprisingly, the poetic and bardic traditions of this period also featured stories of wars, warriors, and sieges. As we have already noted in Chapter 2, evidence for oral poetry in Greek stretches back to the Bronze Age. What we can discern about the subject matter of this poetry suggests that at least some of it focused on martial themes: warrior iconography is characteristic of the Mycenaean palaces, and images of sieges and naval battles are also known. Such scenes appear to be standardized or stock images, illustrating well-known stories or referring to a wider narrative context that the viewer would have been expected to recognize.[16]

Poetic traditions in Anatolian and Near Eastern languages are also relevant. The Hittite texts include several relevant poems and songs, most notably the Hurro-Hittite *Song of Release*. This poem, recorded bilingually already in the

Late Bronze Age, tells the tale of the destruction of the city of Ebla in the Levant, which was brought about by the anger of the gods following the refusal of the city council to release important prisoners.[17] The parallels with the epics of the Trojan War are obvious – the refusal to release prisoners is similar to Agamemnon's reluctance to return Chryseis to her father; the ensuing wrath of the gods is similar to Apollo's curse on the Achaean army; and the destruction of the city of Ebla is paralleled with the sack of Troy. Mesopotamian epics such as *Gilgamesh* were also known and performed in Hittite centres in Anatolia, featuring comparable scenes of heroic combat.

War was not just a reality of everyday life in the Late Bronze Age Aegean and Anatolia, it was a feature of cultural life as well. In such a context, many stories about both historical and fictional conflicts were told, perhaps sometimes being mixed up and confused along the way. The source material for the Homeric epics, and the Epic Cycle more generally, certainly belongs in this setting.

## The real Trojan War: An eighth-century phenomenon

The Homeric poems belong not to the Late Bronze Age however, but to the Geometric period several centuries later. Traditional stories and old themes were used in the process of Homeric composition, but they were reworked and combined with new elements to create original literary works. While it is possible to identify some of these older components in the poems, we cannot always be sure which parts of the story belong to an eighth-century context and which are earlier.[18]

As we have seen, the evidence suggests that generic stories of warriors and sieges existed before the composition of the *Iliad*. Given the widespread nature of conflict in the Late Bronze and Early Iron Ages, these stories could have been attached to any number of different locations, or may have existed as mythic tropes not linked to specific cities at all. Two vital developments probably date to the eighth century however: the gathering of older stories into a single account of grand coalitions and a great siege, and the choice to locate this siege at Troy.

There are a number of factors that make an eighth-century date for these developments likely. First and most importantly, a sense of collective Greek identity was beginning to emerge. Several factors contributed to this: the emergence of Panhellenic sanctuaries at Delphi and Olympia; the spread of the alphabet creating a new sense of linguistic commonality; and the expansion of Greek settlement and trade across the Mediterranean and Black Sea. A new sense of Greek identity was just beginning to emerge. The Iliadic idea of a grand Achaean alliance fits into these wider developments.[19]

Another relevant development of the eighth century was the development of the Greek city state, or *polis*. This included increased urbanization, the emergence of formal civic structures, and the establishment of laws and the concept of citizenship.[20] Against this background, the concern of the *Iliad* with community organization comes into sharp focus.

The choice to locate the story at Troy also makes sense in an eighth-century setting. One of the areas where Greek settlers were especially active during this period was the Hellespont and the Black Sea – that is, the area around Troy. Greeks were establishing new communities in northwestern Aegean at precisely this time, and beginning to make their first forays through the Dardanelles. At the time that the *Iliad* was composed, it made perfect sense to choose Troy as the setting for a grand story of exploring conflict and reconciliation, community and individualism, identity and fate.

The myth of the Trojan War that we know from Greek epic is, essentially, an eighth-century tale composed in an eighth-century context. It makes use of older legends and oral traditions, some of which may potentially have a historical basis in the Late Bronze and Early Iron Age. But we should not hope to find traces of Hector and Achilles in the archaeology of Troy, or to excavate Helen's bedchamber and uncover the Achaean encampment. To seek such literal parallels between Homeric poetry and the archaeology of Troy would be to miss the point of both.

The archaeology tells us about the realities of life in the city of Troy over the ages, shedding light on how people lived and died in this long-established settlement, poised between the Mediterranean and the Black Sea, at the meeting of Europe and Asia. The poetry of Homer and the Epic Cycle tells us about the hopes, dreams, and concerns of the people and societies who produced that poetry. Both subjects are fascinating in their own right. Where the two come together is in the later history of Troy, after the site had become inextricably linked with the myth. As we shall see in Chapter 7, this seems to have happened relatively quickly after the *Iliad*'s composition.

The poem's popularity spread rapidly across the Mediterranean and Near East. By the seventh century, the general perception of the city of Troy would necessarily have been formed with reference to the Trojan War myth. From this time on, images from myth came to influence the everyday reality of life at Troy, and ideas from Homer shaped the practical place of Troy in the wider world. Troy the myth began to have a crucial impact on Troy the city.

# Part Two

# City

High barrows, without marble or a name,
A vast, untill'd, and mountain-skirted plain,
And Ida in the distance, still the same,
And old Scamander, (if 'tis he) remain;
The situation seem still form'd for fame –
A hundred thousand men might fight again
With ease; but where I sought for Ilion's walls,
The quiet sheep feeds, and the tortoise crawls;

Byron, Troy (Don Juan, Canto iv Stanzas 76–78)

The city of Troy stands at the mouth of the Dardanelles, guarding the narrow straits that connect the Aegean and the Black Sea (Map 1). Although the site now lies several kilometres inland, in antiquity it overlooked a calm bay which provided safe anchorage for ships passing along this crucial trade route (Map 2).

The city itself was originally perched on a natural hill, but rebuilding and occupation over the centuries have meant that this hill eventually grew to become a substantial mound. The mound of Hisarlık, which means 'fortified place' in Turkish, was the citadel of Troy where the most important buildings of the community were located. During several periods, however, there was also a lower city that stretched across the plain beneath the citadel. The city grew and developed over a period of nearly four millennia, changing constantly during this time.

The mound itself is made up of many different levels, from the most recent late Roman levels on the top to the lowest levels of the Early Bronze Age. As we saw in Chapter 3, one of the site's early excavators, Wilhelm Dörpfeld, devised a system of dividing these chronological layers into nine major levels – Troy I–IX. We still use this system today (Map 3).

In this section of the book, we will explore the nine cities of Troy through these nine archaeological levels, beginning with the earliest and ending with the latest. In Chapter 5, we will discover Troy of the Early and Middle Bronze Ages, covering the first five major levels – Troy I–V. This prosperous and expanding settlement was mistaken for Homeric Troy by the site's first excavator, Heinrich Schliemann. We will then turn to the most likely candidate for Homeric Troy in Chapter 6 – Troy VI–VIIa. The splendour of this Late Bronze Age city echoes through the epic tradition, and the very idea of Troy became intrinsically linked with its sophistication and wealth.

The more modest remains of Early Iron Age Troy are the subject of Chapter 7, which explores how myths about the heroic past had already begun to shape the lives of Troy's inhabitants. Myth was already firmly interwoven with civic identity. The legend of Troy was also a crucial factor shaping the city during the Greek period, as we shall see in Chapter 8. In an era where the Greek world was made up of hundreds of disparate city states, the story of the Trojan War found a new significance against a backdrop of an emerging Hellenic identity.

In Chapter 9, we will see how myths became vitally important once more in the Hellenistic period, although this time as a means of articulating political authority rather than civic identity. The monumental rebuilding of Troy in this age of competing kings and rival dynasties brought the city into a new international discourse of power. This developed yet further in the Roman period, and in Chapter 10 we will see how the city's fortunes rose and fell with the political agendas of different emperors. As Romans claimed descent from the refugees of Troy, the city occupied a special place within the Roman imagination as well as within the Roman Empire.

# Early Troy, *c.* 3000–1750 BCE

The origins of Troy are shrouded in mystery. Although the Troad was inhabited in the Neolithic period as early as 6000 BCE, it was not until the start of the Early Bronze Age some 3000 years later that the mound of Hisarlık itself was occupied. It is not difficult to see what would have attracted the first inhabitants to the site. The low rise of the natural hill would have offered good views over the sea, while its location inside a deep bay would have meant that the spot was both sheltered from the elements and defensible from seaborne foes (Map 2).

This chapter introduces the first five cities of Troy, spanning the Early and Middle Bronze Ages. In the wider region, this was a period which saw the first appearance of social complexity and state-level social organization, the expansion of long-distance trade networks, and the establishment of enduring cultural traditions.[1] Troy took part in these wider transformations, and also struck out on its own unique developmental trajectory.

## Troy I (*c.* 3000–2550 BCE)

The first of the city's nine incarnations is known as 'Troy I'. It was established at the start of the Early Bronze Age, and survived some four and a half centuries. During this time, the city underwent almost constant renovation, with excavators so far identifying fourteen different phases of construction.[2] Building works undertaken in later periods have destroyed some of the Troy I remains, but enough has been uncovered to give us a sense of what this first settlement must have been like (Figure 5.1).

The settlement was built straight onto the natural bedrock of a low hill, and comprised a number of different buildings. Several were designed on a megaron plan, consisting of a large rectangular room or hall entered through a smaller anteroom. The megaron is characteristic of both Aegean and Anatolian architecture throughout the Bronze Age. These structures could be both large and imposing, and indeed one such megaron from the very earliest phase of occupation (Room 102) had an inner hall measuring 7.0 × 18.5 m. Although today we might consider Troy I to be more the size of a village than a city (the city walls enclose an area of only around 90 m in diameter), it is evident that this community had both the wealth and the wherewithal to build on a monumental scale.

This monumental scale of construction is evident from the enclosing wall which circled the settlement. This wall, up 2.5 m thick in parts, was built entirely from stone and heavily fortified. These impressive defences may have served to protect the early Trojans from marauding bands of raiders, likely coming from the sea. Equally, they would have been a symbol of the power and the prosperity of the settlement, marking it out as an important centre for the local area.

Very few comparable sites had fortification walls on this scale.[3] Further inland in Anatolia, the settlement walls at Demircihöyük and Küllüoba were made of mudbrick rather than stone, and were designed to control floods rather than as defences.[4] One site which did have fortifications to rival those of Troy was Limantepe, a coastal site south of Troy near the modern city of Izmir. Here, the city walls were stone built to a height of 2.5 m and punctuated by regular buttresses.[5] It is not by chance that coastal sites were more heavily fortified than those further inland. The sea brought opportunities for trade and access to both valuable raw commodities and exotic luxury items. But it also meant a degree of vulnerability. While Troy and Limantepe may have benefitted from their littoral locations, they were also at greater risk because of them.

Troy's maritime outlook at this time is also evident from its material culture. Pottery traditions in Troy I were closely linked to those of the Aegean islands, with especially close parallels found from Thermi on the island of Lesbos and Poliochni on the island of Lemnos. Imports from the Aegean are also common, not only ceramics but also small metal items of copper and bronze. Chipped stone blades have been found, made from the distinctive obsidian that occurs only on the island of Melos. Indeed, during this phase Troy seems to have been oriented primarily westwards towards the Aegean, rather than eastwards towards the Anatolian plateau, leading to Troy I being labelled as a 'maritime culture'.[6] Troy was to maintain this broadly Aegean-focused outlook throughout the Early Bronze Age, forging ever-closer links with its neighbours across the waters in preference to its neighbours overland.

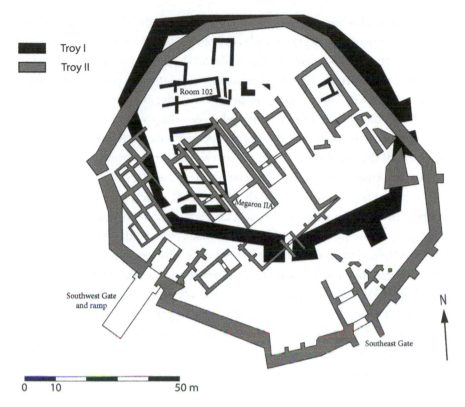

**Figure 5.1** Plan of Troy I and II.

## Troy II (*c.* 2550–2300 BCE)

There was a high degree of cultural continuity between Troy I and Troy II, and it seems that the second city was essentially a remodelling of the first. During this remodelling, the early Trojans took to opportunity to expand their city dramatically and make it even more impressive and monumental (Figure 5.1).[7]

The fortification wall was strengthened and two colossal gateways were built, each flanked by projecting towers. One of these faced inland to the southeast, while the other was approached by a stone-built ramp facing the bay to the southwest (Figure 5.2). The settlement on the mound underwent several different building phases. Its peak was dominated by five particularly large megaron buildings arranged in parallel to each other, the largest of which had an inner hall measuring 20 × 10 m (Megaron IIA). These building were not only conspicuous by their size, but were also physically demarcated by an encircling compound wall, the interior of which had a colonnaded portico.

Traces have also been found of houses beyond the walls. This outer settlement covered an area of nine hectares, and was itself protected by a fortified wooden pallisade. Troy was no longer just the citadel on the mound of Hisarlık, but also comprised the lower city stretching out across the plain. The population of Troy had clearly grown. There must have been a considerable gap in the status of those living outside the citadel walls and those living within them, and then again between everyone else and those with access to the exclusive compound at the centre of the city. For the first time, we can infer the existence of clear class distinctions, enshrined in the physical structure of the city.

The prosperity of this increasingly hierarchical society can be seen in the nature of the finds from the city. In particular, large amounts of metal items were discovered, including finely worked objects made from gold, silver, and bronze. Amongst these finds is the 'Treasure of Priam', a famous collection of precious artefacts that Schliemann claimed to have excavated as a coherent hoard in 1873 (see Chapter 3). Objects from the Treasure include weapons made with cutting-edge bronze technology, splendid metal vessels to grace the tables of the great and the powerful, and fabulous jewellery of the most delicate workmanship (Figure 3.2). Although we now know that these objects came from various different locations on the mound, they are nonetheless still impressive examples of Early Bronze Age metalwork. The wealth of Troy was such that we know of twenty-one different caches of precious metals found in this level.

Another important innovation of the Troy II period was the introduction of the potter's wheel, which allowed for the rapid and efficient manufacture of ceramics on a large scale. This may not quite constitute 'mass production' as we know it, but it certainly led to an upscaling of the industry and the production of a new characteristically 'Trojan' style of pottery. Some of this pottery was made in large enough quantities for export, and Trojan *depas* cups in particular are found widely across Anatolia during this, the Early Bronze II period.

The trade networks which carried the *depas* cups also brought in a wealth of other goods. Crucial amongst these were the large quantities of metal found in Troy II, not only silver and gold, but also copper and tin for the manufacture of bronze. Tin in particular was transported over vast distances to reach Troy, with scientific analysis suggesting that the tin from Anatolian bronzes originated as far away as central Asia.[8] Smaller luxury items also travelled along these networks, and the elites of Troy II wore beads of carnelian and jewellery of lapis lazuli.[9]

It was not just objects and commodities which moved along the great trade routes of the age, but also people, ideas and technologies. Crucially, this interaction led to development of a common elite culture, and in the Early Bronze II period we find similar ways of expressing elite identity and signalling elite status across the Aegean and Anatolia. This included common practices in feasting and the consumption of alcohol, as well as common ways of articulating power through monumental architecture.[10]

Throughout the Aegean and Anatolia, it is possible to trace a significant leap in social complexity at this time: with greater levels of hierarchy and centralization, larger populations concentrated in urban or proto-urban centres, and what has been called an 'International Spirit' stimulated by spiralling connectivity and commerce.[11] It is this period that sees the widespread construction of fortified citadels and monumental central buildings. At sites such as Limantepe and Troy, which already had a history of building works on this large scale, both city walls and central complexes were expanded, becoming even more monumental.[12] At other sites, signs of centralized authority and wealth began to appear for the first time. Inland at Küllüoba for example, the upper town was fortified and administrative complexes and monumental megaron buildings were constructed.[13] Similarly, at Poliochni on the island of Lemnos, the town was strongly fortified and within the settlement walls were built several groups of houses, each clustered around a megaron building.[14]

For all their common elite culture, we cannot assume that the interaction between these communities was always peaceful – indeed, the emphasis on fortifications at both coastal and inland sites would suggest otherwise. The double line of fortifications at Troy also bears witness to the threat of a hostile attack – the city was protected not only by the stone walls of the citadel mound, but also by the wooden palisade which ringed the lower city.

It is possible that an enemy attack was behind the great fire which eventually destroyed the second city of Troy, leaving the citadel in smouldering ruins. This dramatic event led Schliemann to believe that Troy II was the city of Priam and the Trojan War – a theory which has since been disproved by the dating of Troy II to the Early Bronze, rather than the Late Bronze or Early Iron Ages. It is still not clear, however, whether this destruction of the city was due to an enemy attack or to natural causes such as an earthquake. There seem to have been conspicuously few casualties for a violent destruction. Only one skull has been discovered in the burnt debris, and it seems that most of the population was able to escape before the fire took hold. Despite this, it also seems that the inhabitants of Troy II did not return quickly after the conflagration – the hidden caches of precious items were evidently never recovered by their owners.

**Figure 5.2** Partially reconstructed stone ramp leading to Southeastern Gate of Troy II.

## Troy III (*c.* 2300–2200 BCE)

After the prosperity and splendour of Troy III, the third city at Troy is far more modest.[15] On the citadel, the large megaron buildings are replaced by smaller structures, densely packed on the summit of the mound. These buildings seem mostly to have been of a domestic rather than a public nature, and we have yet to discover a major central building that could have been the seat of government or administration.

One marked change from the previous phase is a preference to build entirely in stone, rather than mixed structures of mudbrick on stone foundations. This may have been because the inhabitants of Troy III were more wary of fires following the conflagration which ended Troy II. It is possible that the fortification walls may have been patched up and still usable in places, but no major repairs or expansion works were undertaken. We do not know whether this was because the people of Troy III lacked the funds to embark on such construction work, or because there was less need for fortifications during this period.

After the splendour of Troy II, the poverty of the third city is striking. The material culture of Troy III is, at best, modest. A small number of copper pins have been found, as well as some items made from stone and ceramic. Some cultural continuity is evident, however – the pottery of Troy III is virtually indistinguishable from that of Troy II. This implies a certain level of stability in the city's population, with craftworking traditions remaining unbroken and consumer tastes and sensibilities staying largely constant. There also seems to have been continuity in the general maritime outlook of the city – cultural links and similarities still set Troy primarily within an Aegean, rather than an Anatolian, sphere.

## Troy IV (*c.* 2200–2000 BCE)

This maritime outlook was set to change in the Troy IV period. During this final phase of the Early Bronze Age, we see signs that the city's inhabitants were beginning to look inland towards central Anatolia for their trade links and cultural influences. This happened to such an extent that Troy IV and Troy V are said to have formed an 'Anatolian Troy culture', in contrast to the 'maritime Troy culture' of Troy I–III.[16]

This change may be partly due to the increasing importance of overland trade during this period and in particular to what is known as 'the Great Caravan Route' that crossed Anatolia diagonally from the Troad to Cilicia.[17] Settlements on the Anatolian plateau were especially prosperous at this time, exploiting links with Mesopotamia and the Caucasus.[18] These included the city of Alacahöyük in north central Anatolia, where a number of spectacularly rich tombs have been discovered. The graves were lined with stone and wood, and filled with a wealth of valuable grave goods, including weapons and decorative metal standards, figurines and jewellery in gold, silver, electrum, and copper, and a vast array of ceramic and metal vessels.[19] With such a powerful economic pull from the east, it is perhaps unsurprising that the Trojans began to turn inland.

The inhabitants of Troy IV did not enjoy the same prosperity as their Anatolian neighbours however. Some rebuilding occurred on the citadel mound and the fortification walls were repaired in a few places, but the scale of the construction remained modest. The apparent poverty of Troy IV may be partly due to the poor state of preservation of the archaeological record. In his eagerness to reach the lower levels of the city, Schliemann removed great volumes of soil from the centre of the mound (see Chapter 3). A substantial amount of what originally remained of this level has therefore been irretrievably lost. It seems unlikely, however, that the lost data would have radically altered our understanding of this phase.

## Troy V (*c.* 2000–1750 BCE)

The fifth city of Troy was constructed roughly at the start of the Middle Bronze Age, and marked a new phase in the city's development.[20] Once again, the citadel was ringed by a fortification wall. Within these walls, the quality of the architecture improved. Houses were larger, walls more neatly built, and plans more regular than in the preceding Troy IV phase. There are also signs of houses being built on the plain outside the citadel once more, suggesting that the population was expanding again.

Troy's increasingly strong connections with central Anatolia must have played a part in this newfound prosperity. At around this time, the Anatolian plateau was pulled into the wider orbit of the Old Assyrian Empire, based in northern Mesopotamia. While the Assyrians did not exert any political control over Anatolia, they were extremely active in long-distance trade, and established several permanent trading stations on the Anatolian plateau.[21] Local Anatolian rulers granted protection to these merchant enclaves, and in return benefitted from the taxes they paid and preferential prices on certain commodities, the most important of which were metals. The largest and best known of these Assyrian trading stations was at Kültepe, where excavators have uncovered over 23,000 documents written on clay tablets in Akkadian cuneiform, the language and script of Assyria.[22] These documents offer us an unprecedented window onto the daily concerns of the Assyrian merchants, and include personal letters and legal documents, as well as receipts, accounts, and other trading records.[23]

Through its involvement in the Assyrian trade network, central Anatolia prospered, gaining access to an extensive web of routes which spanned the Near East and central Asia. At the time Anatolia itself was divided into many independent kingdoms, with the capital cities of these autonomous kingdoms rivalling each other in splendour and wealth. The royal palaces at sites such as Beycesultan and Konya Karahöyük, for example, were giant sprawling complexes built over several levels, decorated with fine fresco painting and containing not only costly luxury items but also evidence for complex administrative and bureaucratic systems.[24]

These royal centres are far more impressive than anything we have so far discovered in Troy V, but it is possible that there may once have been a palace, albeit on a slightly smaller scale, in Troy's fifth city. There was clearly some kind of central authority at Troy by this time, which had overseen the expansion of the city and the rebuilding of the fortification walls. It seems likely that this authority would have been based in some kind of central structure on the peak of the mound. As with Troy IV, however, the remains from the central part of the mound during the Troy V period were completely removed by the hasty excavations of Heinrich Schliemann in the nineteenth century.

## The on-site remains of early Troy

Visiting the site today, you can see several of the key features of early Troy, although it is difficult to get a complete sense of the city plans from the remains on site.

A section of the Troy I fortification wall is currently visible towards the centre of the mound at Information Point 5, as well as a projecting bastion that would have guarded the southern gate of the city at this time. The gate itself seems to have been about 2 m wide, making it easily defensible. More of Troy I can be seen at Information Point 7, at the bottom of Schliemann's 'Great Trench'. Part of the fortification wall was uncovered here, as well as a number of parallel stone walls which seem to have been the walls of rectangular houses. To the north of this area can be seen the remains of House 102, an impressive megaron house which was freestanding, in comparison to the houses to its south which shared party walls.

Parts of Troy II can also be viewed onsite. The area around the southwestern gate of the city is relatively well preserved at Information Point 8, where you can view the fortification wall from the outside, with its outer face slightly sloping and standing to a height of 2–3 m. The gate itself was accessed by a well-paved stone ramp, still visible and partially reconstructed (Figure 5.2). Given the impressive nature of the remains when Schliemann excavated this area, he was convinced that he had discovered the 'Scaean Gate' of the *Iliad*, and it was to the west of this gate that he claimed to have discovered the 'Treasure of Priam' (for which, see Chapter 3). However, it seems that that this would have been the smaller of the two gates to the city.

Parts of the larger southeast gate can be viewed under a newly constructed canopy. This gate was originally heavily fortified, with no less than three different bastions clustered around the entrance. Recent excavations have revealed not only the stone foundations, which stand at 0.6–0.8 m high, but also some of the mudbrick superstructure, preserved to a height of nearly 4 m. The gate itself seems to have been constructed in limestone.[25] What can be seen today under the canopy are not, however, the ancient mudbricks. For reasons of conservation, these could not be left exposed to the elements, and so they have been preserved by embedding them within a modern mudbrick reconstruction.[26] These modern mudbricks have been carefully made to replicate as closely as possible the burned nature of the original bricks (which were burned during the conflagration which ended the Troy II phase). The reconstruction includes not just part of the fortification wall, but also a megaron building that stood just within it.[27]

Further to the west, near Information Point 6, the stone foundations of other Troy II structures can be seen. Just inside the southwestern gate lie the foundations of the monumental Megaron IIA, as well as those of the two smaller megaron buildings which flanked it.

No remains of the third, fourth, of fifth cities of Troy can be seen by visiting the site. The remains of these phases have all been removed, either by later construction activity or through excavation. As noted above, it seems that the architecture of these periods was somewhat less substantial and durable than those of Troy I–II, and a great deal less robust than that of the following Troy VI phase, to which we will now turn.

# Troy in the Age of Heroes, *c.* 1750–1180 BCE

The Late Bronze Age (hereafter LBA) saw Troy at its zenith. The city flourished and prospered, its population grew, and its rulers enjoyed both wealth and influence. If the Troy of the *Iliad* has any basis in historical reality, it is to this period that it owes its vision. Troy VI was a city of grandiose mansions and towering city walls, thronged streets and bustling marketplaces, mysterious priests and fearsome warriors. It was the perfect setting for heroic myths.

The archaeological remains of this period are as complex as they are spectacular and are divided into two main levels – Troy VI and Troy VIIa (Figure 6.1). Unfortunately, all archaeological traces of the very centre of the city – the peak of the citadel mound – have been lost. This is due in part to Schliemann's overenthusiasm (see Chapter 3). Much was also lost in the Hellenistic period, when the mound was levelled off to create a flat terrace on which to build a new Temple of Athena (see Chapter 9). If the LBA city ever had a royal palace, all traces of it have now been lost.

This chapter surveys what we know about 'heroic' Troy, examining the archaeology of Troy VI and VIIa. It will also put LBA Troy in its wider context, exploring the wider world of international trade and diplomacy that criss-crossed the Mediterranean during this time.

## The archaeology of Troy VI (*c.* 1750–1300 BCE)

Troy VI spans a period of several centuries, covering the last years of the Middle Bronze Age and most of the LBA. It is subdivided into eight levels (a–h), the last of which, Troy VIh, is most usually associated with Homeric Troy.[1]

Perhaps the most famous remnant of Troy VI is the circuit of impressive fortification walls that surrounded the citadel (Figure 6.2). The area encircled by these walls was now more than double what it had been in previous phases,

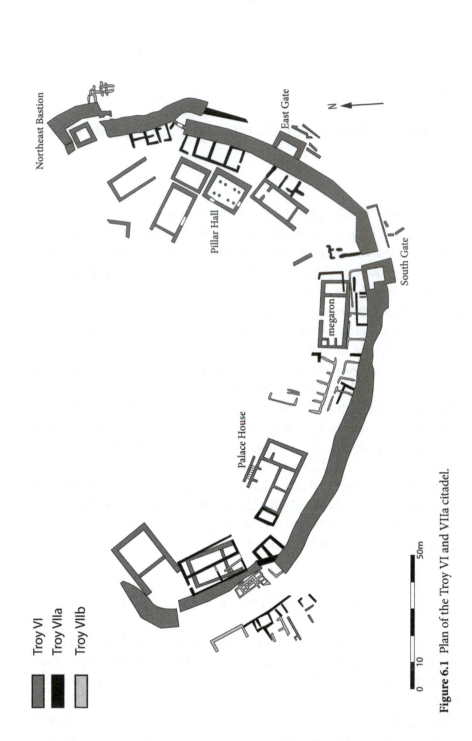

**Figure 6.1** Plan of the Troy VI and VIIa citadel.

at roughly two hectares or 20,000 m². By the fourteenth century, the walls stood at 4–5 m wide and 10 m high, presenting a formidable obstacle to any would-be attacker. To further enhance defensibility, the circuit was punctuated by towers and 'sawtooth' corners.

Within the walls, freestanding buildings stood on a series of terraces rising towards the centre of the mound. They had a wide range of architectural forms, which might indicate competing factions within the city elite. This begins to look more likely when we consider that the buildings were potentially defensible, with thick walls and no ground-floor windows. This is not to say that there was no centralized authority in the city. As mentioned above, any trace of a royal palace would have been lost with the destruction of the central portion of the mound. It is also possible that the different buildings served different functions. The Pillar Hall, for example, contains evidence for textile manufacture and weaving, while the megaron building by the West Gate contained several rich finds, many of a cultic nature (Figure 6.1).[2]

As well as the citadel walls, Troy was protected by fortifications surrounding the lower city. A massive ditch was cut into the bedrock, measuring almost 4 m wide and 2 m deep. This would likely have been combined with a defensive wall, although any traces of this have since been lost due to the erosion of the LBA ground surface. The ditch enclosed an area of about 25–35 hectares, or 250,000–350,000 m². Estimates of Troy's population based on this area range from 4,000 to 10,000 people. By any count, Troy was a large city of the time, and a force to be reckoned with.

After centuries of continuous habitation, Troy VI was dramatically destroyed in its final phase, Troy VIh. Many of the buildings on the citadel were toppled, and there are traces of burning on some parts of the mound. As we saw in Chapter 3, Dörpfeld linked this burnt destruction with the Homeric myth of the Trojan War. We now think, however, that the destruction was caused by a natural disaster, most likely an earthquake. Walls were knocked off their alignments, whole towers in the citadel wall were toppled, and although there were numerous fires across the mound, each seems to have been contained rather than being allowed to spread in an uncontrolled fashion. None of this seems to suggest a violent attack. In addition, very few human remains were discovered in the debris, implying either that people were mostly able to escape before disaster struck, or that dead bodies were later retrieved from the wreckage.

Troy VI was certainly 'Homeric' and 'heroic' in its splendour, and could well have inspired the portrayal of Troy in epic. But the fate of Troy VI was not the fate of Homeric Troy, and the events recounted in epic cannot have been based on the real history of this LBA city.[3]

**Figure 6.2** The walls of the Troy VI citadel.

## The written history of Troy VI

No written records have so far been found in Troy VI. This is surprising, given the size and wealth of the city, and the evident need for an administrative bureaucracy. It is even more surprising, given that throughout the Mediterranean and Near East, the LBA was an era of prolific record-keeping. Archives have been found at the Mycenaean palatial centres of Mycenae, Pylos, Thebes, and Knossos, written in a script known as 'Linear B' and recording an early form of the Ancient Greek language.[4] In Anatolia, archives were kept not only at the Hittite imperial capital of Hattuša, but also at regional centres such as Maşat Höyük.[5] Archives have also been found in the city states of the Levant, most notably at the trading emporium of Ugarit in modern Lebanon.[6] The lack of writing at Troy, then, is puzzling. One possibility is that the archives have been lost or destroyed, likely by Schliemann's hasty excavations. Also possible is that the Trojans wrote on a perishable material which has not been preserved in the archaeological record. After all, a letter from a Hittite King in the mid-thirteenth century mentions wooden writing tablets being sent to the king at Troy.[7]

In the absence of historical documents from Troy itself, we can seek information about the city elsewhere. As we have already seen in Chapter 4, Troy can be identified with a kingdom named 'Wilusa' in the Hittite documents. It is obvious from these texts that there was considerable interaction between the Trojans and the Hittites on the level of diplomacy, politics, and war. The Hittites considered Troy to be an independent principality, a small but important ally on the western fringes of their empire. The earliest reference to Wilusa/Troy in the Hittite sources dates from the sixteenth century BCE, as mentioned in Chapter 4. This fragment of a ritual song suggests that the Hittites knew of epic poetry about the city of Troy. Evocatively, the song begins: 'When they came from steep Wilusa...'[8]

Thereafter, we hear about Troy's activities several times – all, of course, from a Hittite perspective (see also Chapter 4). In the late fifteenth century BCE, Troy joined an alliance of western Anatolian states against the Hittites known as the 'Assuwa Confederacy'.[9] The Hittites, according to their own records, soundly defeated this confederacy, although there is no suggestion that Troy was sacked at this time. Interestingly, the Trojans seem to have made several improvements to their citadel wall and dug the ditch surrounding the lower city at precisely this time.

Thereafter, the rulers of Troy seem to have been on relatively good terms with the Hittites. Indeed, when another coalition against the Hittites sprang up in the fourteenth century, it seems that Troy deliberately chose to stay neutral.[10] This 'Arzawa alliance', as it was known, was primarily composed of principalities in western Anatolia, but also included the kingdom of Ahhiyawa in the Mycenaean Aegean.[11] The precise location of Ahhiyawa within the Aegean remains unclear, but is interesting to note that groups from the Aegean were politically engaged in western Anatolia at this time. For the Trojan elites, the decision to side with the Hittites demonstrated considerable politically savvy. When the Hittite king Mursili II (1321–1295 BCE) eventually defeated the Arzawans, he brought in regime change across the Arzawa states, installing puppet kings who were friendly to his rule.

## Emporium or backwater? The Troy trade controversy

Troy VI was a notable city, with a powerful and warlike ruling class. But what sustained its population, and what supported its fractious elites? It is usually assumed that the wealth of Troy came from commerce, as the city was perfectly placed to profit from interregional trade.[12] However, the extent of Troy's involvement in long-distance exchange remains hotly debated. While some scholars characterize the city as a major hub for interregional connections, others argue that it was relatively insular.[13]

The LBA was a period of unprecedented connectivity, with communities across the Mediterranean and Near East bound together by dense networks of interaction. At the highest level, there were regular contacts between rulers. Hundreds of letters and treaties between LBA kings attest a carefully maintained system of international diplomacy. A particularly important diplomatic archive comes from the Egyptian city of Amarna, including over 300 letters written to and from the Egyptian pharaohs. Some of this correspondence was with independent kings outside of Egypt's sphere of influence, including the kings of the Hittite Empire, Babylonia, Assyria, Mitanni, and Cyprus. These rulers are acknowledged as equals and usually addressed as 'My Brother'. Other letters were written to and from subordinate rulers of Egypt's vassal states usually in the Levant, and contain reports, petitions, and edicts. This high-level diplomatic interaction also involved the movement of luxury goods such as gold, lapis lazuli, and chariot horses, which were exchanged as 'gifts' in substantial quantities.[14]

At another level, mercantile trade flourished. Shipwrecks offer us snapshots of this trade. The Ulu Burun ship, for example, was sunk in the late fourteenth century just off the southwest coast of Anatolia. Its primary cargo seems to have been raw materials (including copper, tin, and blue glass), as well as Canaanite transport jars filled with some kind of organic produce (likely wine or olive oil). But the ship was also carrying substantial quantities of smaller luxury items, including jewellery, weapons, cosmetics, ivory, ebony, ostrich eggs, spices, and miscellaneous pottery.[15] These objects were often made in a hybrid style borrowing elements from many different regions, which can be thought of as an 'International Style'.[16] Merchants like those who owned the Ulu Burun ship could become both wealthy and powerful, and their commerce often overlapped with diplomatic traffic between kings.

Troy's place in this cosmopolitan world is unclear. We know from the Hittite texts that the Trojans engaged with their neighbours both east and west; and from archaeology we know that the city was linked into long-distance mercantile networks, importing gold and ivory luxury items as well as raw metals for the production of bronze. We are still uncertain how well-integrated Troy was within these networks, however, as the archaeological evidence for this is ambiguous.

Several types of object are conspicuous by their absence at Troy. For example, the nearby Mycenaean palaces produced perfumed olive oil in industrial quantities, but little of this seems to have found its way to Troy VI. Similarly,

Hittite ceramics were standard issue throughout the empire and Hittite-influenced areas, but are completely lacking at Troy. Indeed, imported pottery, usually the archaeologists' most reliable source of evidence for external contacts, is rarely found in the city. Instead, Trojans preferred local forms of pottery – developing their own fineware repertoire with first Northwest Anatolian Grey Ware, and later Trojan Tan Ware.[17]

Perhaps the key word in the last sentence is 'preferred'. We know that the Trojans had the opportunity to import foreign pottery if they had wanted to. Instead, it may be that the localism of Troy VI had more to do with consumer choice rather than isolation. Taste, trends, and fashion may have encouraged the Trojans to 'buy local', as well as unwritten social codes about what was deemed desirable and appropriate.

Considering the items exported from Troy, rather than its imports, offers us an alternative window onto Trojan trade. Northwest Anatolian Grey Ware has been found in the Levant and Cyprus, although not in quantities large enough to suggest that they were the primary items of trade. Instead, it has been suggested that Troy's main export business would have focused around textiles. As already mentioned, evidence for textile manufacture has been found on the citadel, but we might reasonably expect most craftworking and production to have happened in the lower city, where more loom weights and spindle whorls have been found. In addition, almost one metric tonne of crushed murex shells has been discovered from Troy VI, suggesting the production of purple dye on an industrial scale.[18] Textiles may, then, have been Troy's main export – a commodity which only rarely survives in the archaeological record. More research is needed, therefore, to investigate the extent and nature of the textiles trade in the LBA.

We also need to know more about trade between the Mediterranean and the Black Sea. Troy's location would have made it a crucial stopping point on this route, but the archaeological evidence for this trade is scanty. Mycenaean pottery and anchors have been found along the Black Sea coastline, implying some trans-Hellespontine connections. But it is impossible to judge how important this trade route may have been.[19] We may have to wait until more excavations are undertaken in this area before the Troy trade controversy is finally laid to rest.

## The archaeology of Troy VIIa (*c.* 1300–1180 BCE)

The earthquake that ended Troy VI was a dramatic event, but it did not mark a break in the story of the city. The urban centre was rebuilt almost immediately, with walls reconstructed and stones from the previous VIh phase being reused. There is also widespread continuity in terms of cultural forms and social practices, although the layout of the citadel underwent some changes. There is no reason, therefore, to suggest that there was a change of population. Instead, it seems that after the destruction, the inhabitants of Troy VI simply set about rebuilding the next incarnation of their city, known to us as Troy VIIa (Figure 6.1).[20] Indeed, it has even been suggested that Troy VIIa is really the final phase of the sixth city and should be renamed accordingly.

The reconstruction needed after the earthquake was substantial. On the citadel, walls that had collapsed were rebuilt. However, further walls were also added, with rooms being subdivided, party walls being thrown up, and new buildings being squeezed into the gaps between older structures. It seems that more people were now occupying the citadel, and space was at a premium. In addition, storage facilities were installed at the lower levels of many houses, in the form of giant pithos jars sunk into the floors. This implies that the inhabitants of Troy VIIa were concerned with their food supply, keen to stock up in case of trouble.

This sense of a community under stress is also evident from the fortifications. In the citadel wall, one gate was sealed; the narrow entrance passageway to another was lengthened; and an additional defensive tower was added to the third. The ditch that defended the lower city was extended so that an even larger area was protected. Not only were more people seeking shelter within the citadel, resulting in some cramped and less-than-luxurious conditions, but they were also coming to the lower city, presumably from the surrounding countryside. Security was clearly a concern.

The remodelling of the city was an ongoing process. Troy VIIa contains two distinct subphases, the second following the trends set in the first for denser occupation and greater security. The finds from these two subphases are much the same as in the previous Troy VI levels, with the ceramic assemblage continuing largely unchanged. One notable difference is a reduction in the already-small quantities of imported Mycenaean pottery. This might imply some shift in economic activity or trading networks, although the characteristic Northwest Anatolian Grey Ware was still exported to the Near East. It is unclear if and how any such socio-economic shifts might have related to the tense security situation. Indeed, while the archaeology of the city can tell us much about *how* life changed in Troy VIIa, it offers us precious few clues as to *why* it did so. To answer this question, we must turn to the historical sources.

## The written history of Troy VIIa

What might have caused the climate of fear that pervaded Troy VIIa? Once more, the Hittite sources are helpful. They suggest that the thirteenth century was a time of great instability, both within western Anatolia as a whole and at Troy specifically.

In the first half of the century, a rogue Arzawan nobleman named Piyamaradu appears several times in the Hittite texts, raiding and seizing land in western Anatolia.[21] He was based in a city called Milawata or Millawanda, likely the precursor of the city later known as Miletus. We hear that Piyamaradu took control of Wilusa/Troy, resulting in the Hittite king leading a campaign to expel him. It is not clear whether either army reached the city of Troy itself, as battles could just have easily been fought in the wider territory of Wilusa. In any case, there are no signs of the city being violently destroyed during the thirteenth century.

The Hittites were likely obliged to come to the aid of Troy by the terms of an alliance with the king of Wilusa. A treaty ratifying this alliance has been discovered in the Hittite imperial archives and has received much scholarly attention because of the name of the Wilusan king involved – Alaksandu. This name is extremely similar to 'Alexandros', an alternative name given to Paris in the *Iliad*. While this does not constitute evidence for the historicity of the Trojan War myth itself, it nonetheless demonstrates that the mythic tradition preserved some elements of real historical information.[22] In seeking a formal alliance with the Hittites, the Trojans may have been hoping for protection from Piyamaradu, but perhaps also from his western allies.

These western allies likely included one or more of the palace states of the Aegean. Piyamaradu's activities were supported by the kingdom of Ahhiyawa, which must be located somewhere in the Mycenaean Aegean. At one point, the Hittite King wrote a frustrated letter to the Ahhiyawan king, complaining about Piyamaradu's troublemaking.[23] At one point, the letter mentions tension between the Hittites and the Ahhiyawans over Wilusa. This tantalizing reference to hostilities between an Aegean-based power and an Anatolian-based power over Troy is an attractive hook for those seeking to ground the Homeric poems in historical truth. We must, however, be wary of reading too much into the source material. The history of Hittite-Ahhiyawan relations does not match the legend of the Trojan War. There is no sign of destruction of conflict at Troy itself during this time, and the Hittites eventually defeated Piyamaradu and made an alliance with Ahhiyawa.

External invasions were not the only threat that faced Troy. Internal strife and political factionalism raged within the city. Towards the end of the century, Walmu, the king of Wilusa, was deposed, only to be rapidly reinstated with the help of the Hittite king. It seems that although the Trojan kings were on good terms with the Hittites, some of their subjects disagreed with this pro-Hittite policy. Civil strife was not completely unexpected. The Alaksandu Treaty explicitly provides for support in cases of internal as well as external threat, and is framed primarily as an agreement between the ruling dynasties rather than between states.

Marked by internal factions, marauding raiders, and Hittite pressure, the thirteenth century was a period of great instability at Troy. The overwhelming concern for security we see in the remains of Troy VIIa must have been a reaction to these troubled times. But, as we shall soon see, more trouble was on its way.

## The on-site remains of heroic Troy

The Troy VI citadel walls loom high above the tourists of today as they must have loomed above the city's attackers. The visitor route around the site begins with a dramatic vista at Information Point 2 overlooking the eastern stretch of the wall, a rectangular tower, and the East Gate. At this point, the wall still stands around 6 m tall and 4.5–5 m thick. Following the route down from the viewpoint leads you directly to the walls themselves, and through the eastern gate.

This gate was not a monumental doorway for making grand entrances into the city. Rather, it was designed for defensibility and the control of access. A narrow passageway is flanked on either side by the sheer slope of the walls, and this must be walked through in order to enter the city. As the East Gate faced the landward side of the citadel, we might imagine that this may have been the side most at risk from attack. The other gates were only slightly less fortified. The South Gate, opening directly onto the lower town, was guarded by a strong tower, the remains of which still stand at 2 m high and can be seen from Information Point 12.

A particularly impressive point of the citadel fortifications can be seen at Information Point 3 – the Northeast Bastion. At 18 × 8 m in size, this bastion was the largest and most imposing of the Troy VI fortification towers. Encased within it was a deep well, which must have been crucial for the survival of the city in a siege situation. Although the bastion today only stands at 7 m tall, it would originally have been at least 9 m in height.

It is somewhat harder to see the remains of the houses and buildings within the citadel. Looking from the vantage point at the start of the visitor route at Information Point 2, it is possible to discern some plans of houses behind the eastern portion of the citadel wall. These include some solidly built rectangular houses from the Troy VI phase, and two more lightly built multiroom structures of Troy VIIa squeezed between the Troy VI houses and citadel well. The houses from Troy VI, sometimes referred to as 'palaces', seem to have been aligned radially from the centre of the citadel and clearly present a stark contrast with the Troy VIIa houses by the thickness of their walls.

At Information Point 9, another Troy VI house can be seen – the structure known as the 'Palace House'. The building's name derives not just from the richness of its finds but also from the high-quality workmanship of its masonry. A final Troy VI building can be seen at Information Point 12, behind the remains of the South Gate. This is the 'Pillar Hall', so named for the pillars supporting the roof inside the central room of the structure and known as a centre for textile production.

Little of the lower city is visible today. Most of the excavations were backfilled, but there are sometimes some remains uncovered to the southwest of the citadel. Also in this direction lies the path which leads to the Spring Cave. The spring was itself located underground, and access was through a narrow passageway cut some 160 m into the living rock. There were also no less than four shafts cut upwards to the surface from this passageway, with a height of up to 17 m. The Spring Cave is not itself a construction of the Late Bronze Age, but seems to have been in use from the Early Bronze Age onwards. But it is for the LBA that the spring is best known, as it is likely to have served a ritual as well as a practical function at this time. In the treaty between the Hittite King Muwatalli II and Alaksandu of Wilusa, oaths are sworn by the deity Kaskal.Kur, the 'god of the underground water-course'. Although we cannot be sure, it seems likely that this underground spring was the location of the cult.

## Postscript: The end of the world (order) is nigh

The fear and instability of the thirteenth century came to a dramatic climax in the early twelfth century. Troy VIIa was destroyed by a sudden attack, resulting in the burning and demolition of the city.

In comparison to previous destruction levels, the evidence for violence at this point is compelling. The remains of the city are covered in a thick layer of ash, indicating that a fierce conflagration was involved. At some points, this layer of ash is as much as a metre thick, giving us some sense of the ferocity of the blaze. In addition, there are unburied human remains in the debris, and bronze arrowheads and slingshots have been found in the area just outside the citadel that would later become the West Sanctuary (Figure 8.1).

Carl Blegen, who led the excavations at Troy in the 1930s, felt that this must surely be the archaeological footprint of the Trojan War. Leading up to the destruction of the city, there had been a worsening of relations with the Aegean, manifested in the reduced trade in Mycenaean pottery. This, Blegen felt, could have eventually culminated in an attack by a combined Aegean force on Troy. Blegen's theory is appealing but problematic. The destruction dates to the early twelfth century, between 1180 and 1150 BCE. By this time, the Mycenaean palace states of the Aegean had already collapsed and, therefore, could not have launched a military campaign against Troy. Whoever did burn the city, it was certainly not a coalition of kings and princes from the Aegean. So what *did* happen to Troy VIIa?

Crucially, the events at Troy were no isolated phenomenon. All around the eastern Mediterranean, kingdoms were collapsing and settlements were being destroyed, all at roughly the same time.[24] In the Aegean, the Mycenaean palaces were burnt and abandoned. In central Anatolia, the Hittite Empire collapsed and the capital city left largely derelict. In the Levant, many important urban centres also suffered burnt destructions and were never rebuilt. Egypt was riven by dynastic wars and lost its imperial possessions.

Everywhere you looked, the carefully balanced world order of the LBA, with its complex diplomacy and vibrant trade, was crumbling. How this came to pass, and what brave new world emerged from the ashes, we shall see in the next chapter.

# Troy in the 'Dark Age', *c.* 1180–900 BCE

The Late Bronze Age (hereafter LBA) was an era of Great Kings and vast empires, monumental architecture and fine arts, connectivity and cosmopolitanism. The peoples of the Mediterranean and Near East were tied into a vast, complex, and sophisticated world order. This world order came crashing down around the end of the thirteenth century BCE. Why this happened and what happened afterwards are the focus of this chapter.

Troy, like many other cities across the region, suffered a dramatic violent destruction *c.* 1180 BCE. The occupation level after this destruction is known as Troy VIIb, and is divided into three main subphases: Troy VIIb$_1$, Troy VIIb$_2$, and Troy VIIb$_3$. These subphases span what is commonly known as the 'Dark Age', but which should more accurately be referred to as the 'Early Iron Age' (hereafter EIA).

The EIA was a time of more modest living standards, reduced connectivity, and fluid sociopolitical structures. Centralized states gave way to more egalitarian communities, with the result that many things associated with elite culture disappeared. There was a decrease in writing, a reduction in the number and scale of public buildings, and a drop in the production of luxury items and elite goods. As a result, some scholars have characterized this period as a 'Dark Age' of backwardness and barbarity. But the darkness has more to do with our lack of knowledge than with any real decline in civilization. The very things that we rely on to learn about the ancient past – written records and durable archaeological remains – are usually connected to elite activity. As a result, we know relatively little about periods such as the EIA, when these elites had lost their power.

EIA society may have been poorer and less stable than its predecessor, but it was also more flexible. This flexibility afforded new opportunities and allowed new social and cultural configurations to emerge. One of these new configurations eventually became what we now call 'the Greek world' (which we will explore in Chapter 8). Shared stories and common myths played a vital role in the emergence of the Greek world, and the myths of Troy were vital among them. These myths, as we can see from the remains of EIA Troy, had already begun to take shape almost before the ashes of the LBA city had settled.

## Catastrophe and collapse: The end of the Late Bronze Age

As we saw in Chapter 6, the end of the LBA across the eastern Mediterranean and Near East was marked by violence, collapse, destruction, and chaos. Great kingdoms fell, powerful dynasties were snuffed out, and entire cities were reduced to rubble. What happened, and why?

These questions still generate heated debate.[1] For many years, scholars maintained that marauding invaders were the agents of this apocalypse. These invaders were thought to have swept down from continental Europe, cutting a swathe of death and destruction through mainland Greece, and an episode that is thought to lie behind the later Greek myth as the 'Dorian Invasion'. These incomers and the peoples they had displaced supposedly then took to the water, raiding around the Mediterranean and causing the collapse of individual states as well as of the international system. By this point, the piratical invaders are usually referred to as 'The Sea Peoples' – a modern umbrella term which has been applied to nine distinct groups mentioned in Egyptian sources. According to this traditional perspective therefore, the end of the LBA can be explained by external migration and sudden invasion.

There is certainly evidence for piracy and seaborne raids around this time. Writing to the King of Cyprus, the King of Ugarit begged for help against raiders who were attacking towns on the Levantine coast. His tone is desperate: 'enemy ships came and burned my towns with fire. They have done evil things in the land!.... the country is lying abandoned!'[2] This documentary evidence for raiders, coupled with later traditions about invaders, seems to offer a neat explanation for the cities sacked and the kingdoms toppled.

The theory may be attractive in its simplicity, but it is also problematic. The idea of the Dorian Invasion of Greece actually dates to the nineteenth century, and has no real basis in the ancient texts. The idea of the Sea People is also a modern construct. In the Egyptian texts, different groups were active at different times, and only three of the nine named groups are designated as being 'of the sea'. On close examination, the texts do not match as neatly with the archaeological evidence as we might want them to.

Most scholars would now agree that the collapse of LBA society was far more complicated than the 'migrant invader' theory allows. For the real causes of collapse, we need to look closer to home. The international system that supported the kingdoms of the LBA was precariously balanced. It relied on a delicate equilibrium between local and imperial powers, elites and productive groups, rulers and the ruled. The interconnections were such that states and dynasties depended on each other to maintain power – economically, militarily, and ideologically. Once one domino fell, it was only a matter of time before the rest would inevitably tumble.

When we examine the end of the LBA in detail, it emerges that the catastrophe was less sudden and simultaneous than initially assumed. The collapses actually occurred over a period of about fifty to eighty years. Some destructions, like those of the Mycenaean palaces, happened in the final decades of the thirteenth century; while others, such as that of Troy, occurred in the first half of the twelfth. We are not, therefore, seeking to explain an event so much as a process.

We also know from our examination of Troy VIIa that the thirteenth century was a time of war and instability. This instability stretched far beyond Troy. During the thirteenth century, the Hittite Empire faced intense dynastic conflicts, with uncles usurping nephews and illegitimate children claiming the throne. In addition, key territories threw off imperial rule, with some local potentates even challenging Hittite authority by assuming the title 'Great King'.[3] A similar phenomenon can be seen in Egypt, where the Nineteenth Dynasty collapsed inwards through dynastic infighting. Perhaps unsurprisingly, the vassal states in the Levant took this opportunity to secede, and Egypt lost its imperial possessions. By the end of the thirteenth century, the great powers of the LBA were already on the decline. All that was needed to tip the balance was a shock to the system.

Such a shock may have come from the bottom, rather than the top of the social pyramid. The entire LBA system depended on the production of substantial surpluses by the working population, and there is evidence to suggest that in the latter thirteenth century this was no longer possible. Paleoenvironmental data suggests that there was climate change and prolonged drought around this time, which would likely have led to famine.[4] Such conditions would create large numbers of disaffected people, perhaps wandering or transient populations, who might well take recourse to raiding and piracy. The people involved in these activities need not necessarily be a coherent army of invaders from abroad, but could simply have been bands of desperate or opportunistic individuals.[5]

An inherently unstable system, already disintegrating through political intrigue and rivalry, was put under yet more pressure by environmental shocks and climate change. Increasing competition for resources would have led to the rise of rootless and mobile groups, and as state authority dwindled, we might imagine a gradual breakdown in the rule of law. The pirates that threatened Ugarit were probably not a coherent colonizing force of 'Sea Peoples', and the attackers that burned Troy were probably not an organized migrant population. It was problems within that made the system vulnerable to shocks from without, and both insiders and outsiders must have been responsible for the violence and chaos that ensued.

At Troy, the destruction was dramatic and the collapse total. But from the debris and the ashes, a new order was about to emerge.

## The reoccupation of Troy VIIb₁ (*c.* 1180–1120 BCE)

After the destruction of Troy VIIa, the occupants of the city returned almost immediately to build the VIIb₁ phase. Troy VIIb₁ lasted perhaps no longer than around sixty years, and its archaeological traces are scanty. Houses seem to have been rebuilt only on the citadel, while finds in the lower town consist solely of pits and a refuse ditch. It seems, therefore, that there was a substantial decrease in the city's population. Unsurprisingly, given their recent experiences, security continued to be a concern – the East Gate to the citadel was completely sealed off during this phase.

There are two main changes in the material culture of the city that can be identified from the evidence available. The first change is that the large pithos jars which characterized Troy VIIa went out of use suddenly. Perhaps the inhabitants opted for other means of storing supplies, or perhaps it was no longer so easy to build up stores in the first place. The second change is the introduction of a new type of burnished pottery, similar in many respects to pottery from the Balkans. This new handmade ware was used for cooking vessels and small storage pots. Dining and drinking vessels were still made in the traditional Trojan grey and tan wheel-made wares.

The VIIb₁ level has turned up one especially interesting find which demonstrates continuity with heroic Troy.[6] This is a bronze biconvex seal, inscribed with Luwian hieroglyphs (Figure 7.1). The language of Luwian seems to have been spoken widely across much of LBA Anatolia, but the hieroglyphic script was particularly associated with the Hittite administration. It is therefore remarkable that this object, with its associations of Hittite imperial bureaucracy, should appear in an EIA level at Troy. The seal may have been an heirloom, passed through generations of Trojans. Equally, it may have arrived at Troy during this phase, brought here by someone fleeing the fall of Hattuša.

**Figure 7.1** Bronze biconvex seal with inscription in Luwian hieroglyphs.

## The rebuilding of Troy VIIb$_2$ (*c.* 1120–1050 BCE)

Troy VIIb$_2$ is characterized by more energetic rebuilding activity.[7] In this period, more houses were built on the citadel, storage facilities were constructed immediately outside the citadel walls, and the lower town was once again inhabited. Although most of the buildings were built in wattle and daub, the few made from stone exhibit some dramatic new features. In particular, orthostats became popular, having been only rarely used in previous phases. Changes in the ceramic assemblage are even more marked, with a notable increase in the amount of new handmade wares, and in the range of their vessel shapes and functions.

It has been suggested that these changes mark the arrival of a new immigrant population from the Balkans, who brought the new styles and technologies with them. These incomers have been linked with the Phrygians, a later Iron Age population whose state was based at the city of Gordion and who appear in Greek myth as the people of the hapless King Midas.[8] The evidence does not suggest a mass migration or wholesale supplanting of the Trojan population – grey and tan wheelmade wares are still produced, for example. However, the collapse of old trade networks may have opened up opportunities for new links northwards. People, ideas, and influences may therefore have come to Troy by these means.

Troy VIIb$_2$ ended with a destruction horizon *c.* 1050 BCE, which seems likely to have been caused by another earthquake. Rubble and fallen masonry has been found across the site, but the population seems to have been able to clear out many of their possessions from the collapsed structures. The abandonment of the Troy VIIb$_2$ houses was therefore a careful and deliberate act, with the rooms thoroughly cleaned before they were finally deserted. This rather abrupt end of Troy VIIb$_2$ remains something of a mystery. Why did the population not rebuild? Where did they go afterwards?

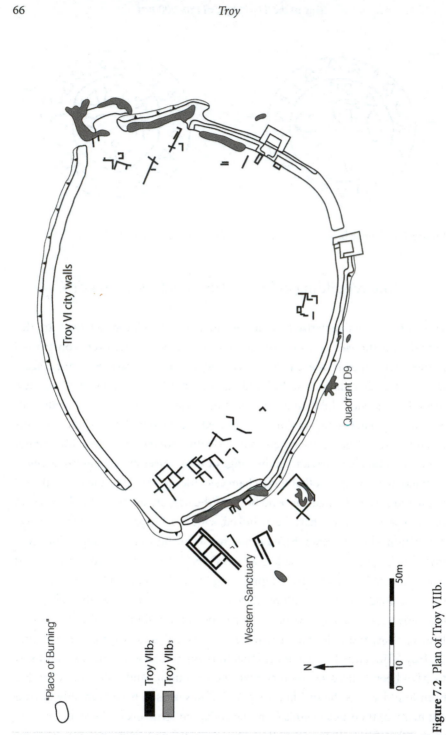

**Figure 7.2** Plan of Troy VIIb.

## The beginnings of myth in Troy VIIb₃ (*c.* 1050–900 BCE)

For much of the twentieth century, we assumed that Troy was unoccupied for many generations after the abandonment of Troy VIIb₂. Only recently has ceramic material been found that can be securely dated to the period immediately afterwards, leading to the identification of a new level – Troy VIIb₃.[9] This crucial evidence has come in the form of protogeometric pottery, a style of ceramics best known from mainland Greece and from Athens in particular. Although protogeometric pottery constituted only a small proportion of the ceramic assemblage at Troy, it is still vital in helping to establish a date for the phase as a whole.

The protogeometric pottery found in northwestern Anatolia has traditionally been linked with the idea of the 'Aeolian Migration'. This was a mythic migration of Greek-speaking people from the western Aegean, reportedly led by Orestes after he was exiled from Mycenae for killing his mother Clytemnestra, in vengeance for the death of his father Agamemnon. Recent research has established that there is little evidence for this myth having any historical basis. Indeed, the absolute quantities of protogeometric pottery in the Troad do not imply a large-scale migrant population.[10]

As yet, no buildings have been uncovered from Troy VIIb₃, but evidence has been found for ritual activity at several locations. These include the ruins of an abandoned LBA building in an area outside the city walls known as the Western Sanctuary, and an area just outside the southern stretch of the citadel wall in the excavation Quadrant D9 (Figure 7.2). The building in the Western Sanctuary had been destroyed at the end of Troy VIIa, and had lain abandoned for a period of 100 years or so (Figure 8.1). Now however, people began to dig pits in and around the remains of the structure, depositing within them caches of cultic objects. These included burned animal bones, amphorae and drinking vessels, and ornate incense burners. The remains in Quadrant D9 are similar.

The location of this cult activity cannot have been accidental. In the case of Quadrant D9, the citadel wall would still have been visible, partially collapsed at the top but still looming high above the plain. A terrace was built here, creating a raised platform at the base of the wall upon which rituals could be enacted. These rituals must have been directed, literally as well as symbolically, at the imposing remains of a glorious and heroic past. In the Western Sanctuary, the physical remnants of the past would have been less immediately visible, but some kind of cultural memory of the building must have been passed down through the generations enabling the people of Troy VIIb₃ to successfully relocate it.

We have yet to discover any domestic deposits from this phase. So while we know that there were people at the site of Troy, we do not know where they lived. It is possible that they settled at the top of the citadel mound, and that the remains of their houses have since been destroyed. Alternatively, people may have chosen to live on the plain, in areas which have not yet been archaeologically explored.

Whoever these people were, and wherever they lived, they were keen to link themselves to the ancient past. The remains of VIIb$_3$ suggest that oral traditions, stories, and mytho-historic knowledge about Troy's history were transmitted through the centuries. Indeed, the physical traces of the glorious past would have been ever-present for the EIA occupants of the site – the citadel walls, if nothing else, stood testament to the lost glory of the ancient city.

## The Trojan 'Dark Age'?

EIA Troy does indeed seem 'dark' to us, in that its history and its people are obscured from our view. But there is more going on here than initially meets the eye. In this, Troy is a good illustration of current thinking about the so-called 'Dark Age'.

The Trojans of this period may not have had the wealth of their predecessors, but there is much to say about them nonetheless. Troy was a dynamic and changing community, with new links opening up with continental Europe and the western Aegean, and new people coming to the city. There was also continuity with previous phases. The continued use of LBA objects such as the Luwian seal implies some knowledge of the past. The deliberate location of ritual activity to incorporate LBA remains is also crucial. For the people of Troy VIIb, the heroic past was not just history; it was an essential part of their present identity. From these early beginnings, the mythic past rapidly came to dominate the city of Troy and its people.

## The on-site remains of Dark Age Troy

There is little to see on-site today of the remains of Troy VIIb. The material was so disturbed and scanty that very little was preserved beyond excavation. The one exception to this is the area of the West Sanctuary at Information Point 10. Depending on the state of vegetation and the time of the year, it may just be possible to see some of the walls of the early cult buildings (Figure 8.1).

# Troy in the Greek World, *c.* 900–335 BCE

The Early Iron Age was a time of instability and transformation, but also of opportunity. This allowed for the gradual development of a conscious Hellenic identity and the emergence of what we now know as the Greek world.

This world comprised many hundreds of autonomous states, usually focused around individual cities. While the Greek world had the Aegean at its heart, its communities were geographically scattered from Marseille to Cyprus, Libya to the Black Sea. What held these disparate populations together was their conscious self-identification as being 'Greek', and their engagement in a common set of cultural norms. These included speaking a dialect of the ancient Greek language, sharing similar religious and cultic systems, and engaging with a shared pool of mythic traditions which created a sense of a common past.

Troy played a crucial role in this latter phenomenon, and myths about Troy were fundamental in the making of Greek identity. This was true at the level of individual Greek cities, as many traced their foundation myths back to the heroes of the Trojan War; but also at the Panhellenic level, as the ideal of collective Greek action was projected back onto the Achaean host.

In this chapter, we will see how stories of Troy forged the Greek world, and also explore the most of the remains of the eighth city. Troy VIII can be divided into several phases, which roughly correspond to the Geometric (*c.* 900–650 BCE), Archaic (*c.* 650–480 BCE), and Classical (480–330 BCE) periods. The final phase of Troy VIII was the massive remodelling undertaken in the Hellenistic period, which we will consider in Chapter 9.

## The archaeology of Geometric Troy (*c.* 900–650 BCE)

The ninth, eighth, and first half of the seventh century at Troy are not well preserved in the archaeological record.[1] As with previous levels, the remains at the centre of the mound have been lost, and do not seem to have been particularly extensive in the first place. Once again, the Western Sanctuary currently offers the best-preserved archaeology, and so, once again, we know more about the ritual life of Troy's inhabitants than about their domestic arrangements (Figure 8.1).[2]

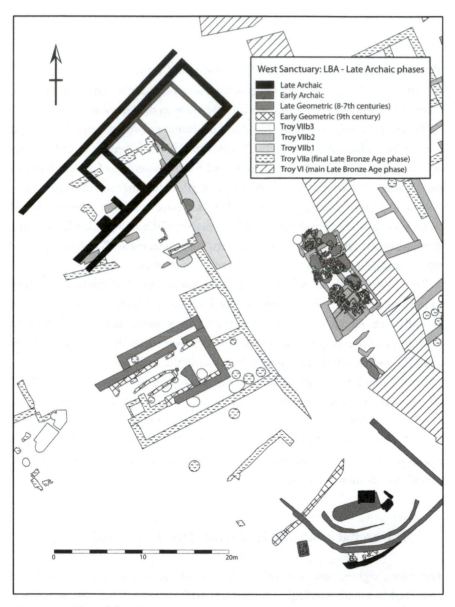

**Figure 8.1** Plan of the Western Sanctuary.

The remains of a Late Bronze Age house was the setting for ritual activity during Troy VIIb$_3$ (see Chapter 7). A new structure was built in the ninth century, making use of three surviving Late Bronze Age walls, but incorporating them into a novel plan. This featured a long central room, inside which were an apsidal altar and a statue base. This building was extended and remodelled in the late eighth or early seventh century, when it became part of a wider cult complex. Directly to the north, a series of hearths and post holes suggest another structure, made of timber rather than of stone. In addition, a large platform was constructed abutting the citadel wall, on which were twenty-eight paved stone circles, each measuring about 2 m in diameter. There were traces of burning on them, and the ceramics found suggest feasting. The rituals here must have been somewhat theatrical – eating and drinking by the light of roaring fires, raised high up on a platform against the backdrop of the Bronze Age city walls.

Evidence for similar rituals can be found in an area about 90 m northwest of the citadel, at a location that Carl Blegen called the 'Place of Burning' (Figure 7.2).[3] The evocative name points to the presence of burned human remains, found in some fifty or so cremation urns dating to the Late Bronze Age. These antiques (as they would have been for the Geometric period inhabitants of the city) were incorporated into rituals held in a large oval building constructed *c.* 700 BCE, rituals which also involved feasting. Traces of similar rituals have been found once more in Quadrant D9, in an area against the citadel wall that had previously seen cult activity in Troy VIIb$_3$.[4] In this phase, a new structure was built directly alongside the citadel wall, and ritual activity associated with feasting continued.

How should we interpret this apparent obsession with the heroic past at Troy? On one hand, the Trojans of the Geometric period were simply continuing traditions that had begun in the Early Iron Age. On the other hand, there was a major increase in this activity in the eighth and seventh centuries. What caused this sudden obsession with ancient history?

At this time, Troy was expanding its maritime networks, and began to dominate the economic activities of its immediate neighbours. Crucially, the city began to export a new type of tan coloured fineware pottery, across the northern Aegean. This ramping up of trade may also be linked to the growing power of the Anatolian kingdoms further inland. First Phrygia and later Lydia were to dominate the Anatolian interior, creating new markets for luxury goods and exerting new political pressures on their borders. But the intensification of interest in the Trojan past must owe primarily to the dramatic changes under way in the wider Greek world.

## Troy and the expansion of the Greek world

In the Geometric age, the Greek world as we know it was coming into being. As we saw in Chapter 2, the *polis* or city state was gradually emerging, and communities were just beginning to identify themselves as Athenians, Spartans, Thebans, etc. At the same time, Greeks started to trade widely throughout the Mediterranean and Black Sea, often settling and creating new communities in the lands that they visited. This latter phenomenon, conventionally known as Greek 'colonization', brought Greeks into contact with a wide range of new peoples and places. The Geometric period was a time of mobility and adventure, as well as of settlement and the formation of new communities.

Around this time, Greeks began to show an increased interest in the past. On the Greek mainland, shrines were being erected at Mycenaean sites and monumental Bronze Age tombs were honoured as the resting places of mythic heroes. With new cities and societies being built, there was an impulse to look back to an age of heroic ancestors.[5] Stories of these ancestors must have circulated widely.

It can be no accident that the Homeric epics were composed at precisely this time. The *Iliad* was first set down in writing during the late eighth century, and the *Odyssey* not long after. The appeal of epic poetry, telling tales of the glorious past, must have been considerable in this time of radical social change. Indeed, we know that Homeric epic was wildly popular, and the poems were instant hits almost as soon as they were composed. We have already encountered the first visual depiction of the Troy story on a pithos from Mykonos (Figure 2.2), but there is evidence that the Homeric version of the myth was particularly widely known.

Within a few years of the *Iliad* being composed, a young boy was buried at the site of Pithekoussai on the island of Ischia in the Bay of Naples. Pithekoussai was one of the earliest of the new Greek communities to be established in the central Mediterranean, and this boy must have been amongst the first new generation of children born at the site. Amongst the gifts laid in his grave was a drinking cup made on Rhodes, adorned with one of the earliest inscriptions known in alphabetic Greek. The form of the lettering is from the Aegean island of Euboea, but the inscription was likely made at Pithekoussai itself as some western Greek letters were also used. The inscribed text is a rather surprising short poem, written in the epic hexameter form.

> I am Nestor's cup, good to drink from;
> Whoever drinks from this cup, he will immediately
> Be seized by the desire of beautiful-crowed Aphrodite.

It may seem strange to us that a verse dealing with alcohol and sex should be found in the grave of a child, but perhaps a more important clue as to the cup's significance can be found in the poem's first line. The mention of Nestor's cup is an explicit reference to a passage from the *Iliad* (Book 11.632-7), implying that the Homeric epic was known at Pithekoussai. For the bereaved community, burying this boy with the cup of Nestor was a way of marking his elite status, and sending him on his way to a heroic afterlife. The inscription also demonstrates that the myth of Troy had spread far and fast, providing a common cultural touchstone for Greek communities across the Mediterranean.

It also offered them a way to conceptualize a shared past. Not long after the Homeric poems were composed, another epic poem in the Greek Epic Cycle was written – the *Nostoi* (literally: 'The Returns'). This poem dealt with the stories of Achaean heroes returning after the end of the Trojan War, with the twist that very few of them made it home at all. Instead, the poem told of their wanderings far and wide, and explained how many of them founded new cities during their travels. The tales of the *nostoi* played to the needs of the moment – they provided the new Greek communities with foundation myths and stories of origin. Some communities in the central Mediterranean, for example, claim to have been founded by the Achaean hero Diomedes or by Odysseus during his ten-year journey home to Ithaca.[6] The myth of Troy was not just a thread that connected the cultural life of the expanding Greek world, but also an opportunity to create the sense of a common history.

## The archaeology of Archaic Troy (*c.* 650–499 BCE)

The mid-seventh century was another crucial cut-off point in Trojan history, marked by a major destruction horizon. It is not clear whether this destruction owed to natural or human causes, but for the first time there was a brief period of about thirty years when the site was totally abandoned. When the city was rebuilt in the late seventh century, the new structures were constructed on totally new plans and on a new orientation.[7]

Once again, the Western Sanctuary offers some of the best evidence for this phase (Figure 8.1). The area continued to serve a ritual function. The 'Early Archaic Cult Building' consisted of two roughly equal rectangular rooms, and was located on its own terrace. Slightly to the south of this building were two open-air sanctuary areas, each focused on a small altar and demarcated by precinct walls. These are known as the 'Upper Sanctuary' and the 'Lower Sanctuary'. These open-air sanctuaries seem to have been used for making personal dedications, as hundreds of votive items were found in the area. These votives suggest the worship of a female deity, and the involvement of female worshippers in her cult. This mixed ritual area lasted for about a hundred years, until it was dramatically remodelled in the late sixth century. At this point, a monumental stone temple was built on the site, measuring 18 × 8 m, and constructed in the Aeolic order. In front of the temple was an altar, which was gradually expanded over time from 1 m in size to a massive 8 m in length.

There were major new constructions on the citadel as well. Once again, most of these were destroyed either by the Hellenistic builders or by Schliemann, but some traces of them still remain. Specifically, large terraces were built in the late seventh and sixth centuries. These must have supported new domestic areas, as well as an early version of the Temple of Athena. Although this early version of the building was mostly obliterated by the construction of the Hellenistic temple, some of its foundations and a deep ritual well have been discovered.

The changes of the Archaic period went beyond simple rebuilding, however. There was also a degree of social and cultural change. In terms of pottery, local styles of pottery all but disappeared and were replaced by typically Greek wares. These included imports from Athens and Corinth, as well as styles characteristic of the Ionian Greek cities on the coast of Anatolia.[8] In addition, the Greek language began to be used within the city. From the sixth century onwards, a small number of short inscriptions in Greek appear, either as dedications written on votive objects or as graffiti scratched onto pottery.[9]

We should not assume that Troy in this phase had necessarily become a 'Greek' city. On the one hand, its architecture and pottery largely conform to Greek types, and Greek language and script can be seen. At the same time, however, there was continuity in local and Anatolian styles, and the Greek inscriptions found are both rare and brief. Typical practices found in the *polis* are also absent. For example, the city issued no coinage, and there are no public inscriptions set up by the civic authorities. In the wider Troad, there is evidence for hybrid customs in mortuary ritual, and for artistic forms exploiting a range of cultural influences.[10] Troy was certainly engaging with Greek culture and becoming increasingly drawn into the Greek world, but it also maintained its own local flavour.

From the mid-sixth century onwards, the Persian conquest of Anatolia threw yet another element into the mix. The Persians established a regional capital directly to the east of Troy at the site of Daskyleion, and the cultural pull of this centre was felt across the Troad. In economic and political terms, Troy became a second order settlement, falling behind Daskyleion in wealth and importance. By the time the city was hit by yet another earthquake in the late sixth or early fifth century, the myth of Troy was already more powerful than its reality.

## Troy and the Aristocrats

The myth of Troy was already widely known by the start of the Archaic period, acting as a common cultural reference point for the communities of Greeks scattered across the Mediterranean and Black Sea. During the Archaic period, however, the myth acquired a new set of associations, and a more narrowly political significance.

The Trojan War appears frequently in the poetry and art of the Archaic period. Numerous painted vases depicted scenes of Trojan and Achaean heroes in combat (e.g, Figure 8.2). The theme was also taken up in the sculptural decoration of temples and shrines, such as on the Siphnian Treasury at Delphi.[11] Lyric poets such as Sappho, Alcaeus, and Stesichorus not only wrote about the myth of Troy explicitly, but also referred to it in passing, using the Trojan War almost as a byword for heroism and the legendary past. When the poet Ibycus came to write an encomium for Polycrates, the tyrant of Samos, he did so with explicit reference to the heroes of the Trojan War.[12]

**Figure 8.2** Ajax and Glaukos fighting over the dead body of Achilles. Scene from a black-figure amphora, *c.* 540–530 BCE.

But I'm not concerned now with singing of Paris
the cheat-host, nor yet of Cassandra…
Nor yet will I take as my subject
heroes of valour
and pride, whom ships full-bellied,
much-riveted, brought for the downfall
of Troy…
Those topics the skilled Heliconian Muses
could easily cover in story,
but a mere mortal
could never tell the details… [13]

Ibycus, Fragment 263

Ibycus may have been commissioned to write in praise of Polycrates, but he could not sing of heroism, it seems, without making reference to the Trojan War. Indeed, he writes at some length about the myth, all in the frame of explicitly *not* writing about it. Ibycus is playing here with the idea of poetic skill – overtly claiming that only the Muses can recount the tale, while actually recounting it himself and thereby assuming the Muses' mantle. Polycrates also benefits from the lengthy digression – the lustre of heroic Troy necessarily reflects on him.

Ibycus' poem highlights Troy's new significance in the Archaic age. The myth of the Trojan War was crucially associated with not only excellence in valour and heroism, but also excellence in artistic endeavour. It is perhaps unsurprising that the story of Troy became a central part of Greek aristocratic culture, which elevated the pursuit of personal excellence to a way of life. Homeric heroes provided Greek aristocrats with role models for bravery, feats of arms, physical prowess, and morality. They were also co-opted as ancestors for powerful noble families and ruling dynasties. For example, the Philaidae and Alcmaeonidae, two of the most important noble clans of Archaic Athens, claimed descent from Ajax and Nestor, respectively.[14]

The association between the *Iliad*, the myth of Troy, and aristocratic elite culture was close enough that it could be humorously satirized by the final years of the sixth century. One Athenian amphora, painted *c.* 510–500 BCE, depicts a sombre Hector arming for war, flanked by his aging parents Priam and Hecuba (Figure 8.3a). The image offers the viewer a model of correct aristocratic behaviour – a strong and virile young man setting out to do his duty on the battlefield, fighting for his family and community. On the other side of the amphora, however, we are faced with three drunken revellers, presenting a riotous mirror inversion of the Trojan scene (Figure 8.3b). An amphora such as this would have been used to pour wine at a symposium – an all-male drinking party that formed the cornerstone of aristocratic socializing. The painter of this particular amphora, Euthymides, belonged to an avant-garde group of artists who

**Figure 8.3a** Red figure amphora by Euthymides *c.* 510–500 BCE. Side A: Hector arming, flanked by Priam and Hecuba.

**Figure 8.3b** Red figure amphora by Euthymides *c.* 510–500 BCE. Side B: Three drunken revellers.

irreverently subverted social and artistic conventions in their work. Euthymides amphora pokes gentle fun at his aristocratic audience in the symposium – while you might think of yourself as the honourable hero Hector, by the time you reach the bottom of this amphora, you're going to be more like the guys on the other side.

## The archaeology of Classical Troy (499–334 BCE)

The earthquake that devastated Troy towards the end of the Archaic period left much of the city in rubble. For a long time afterwards, there was little reconstruction work; and archaeological remains from the fifth and the fourth century are rare. For some time after the quake, it seems that the Trojans were simply incapable of rebuilding. This can only be partly attributed to the earthquake. The wider geopolitics of the time meant that Troy struggled to recover and took some time to return to its former glory.[15]

Today, we are used to thinking of the Classical period as a golden age for Greeks. Democratic Athens was at its height, and with its austere militarism Sparta too reached the peak of its powers. The Parthenon with its fabulous sculptures dates to this time, as does the Temple of Zeus at Olympia with its chryselephantine statue, one of the seven wonders of the ancient world. The stage rang to the tragedies of Aeschylus, Sophocles, and Euripides, as well as to the comedies of Aristophanes. The events of the age inspired the first historians, Herodotus, Thucydides, and Xenophon; and the philosophers Socrates, Plato, and Aristotle plumbed the depths of human understanding. But the greatness of the Classical age belongs mostly to the cities of the Greek mainland – elsewhere in the Greek world, this was a time of instability and uncertainty.

This was the case for Troy and western Anatolia as a whole. A series of wars raged across the region, allowing its inhabitants little opportunity and even fewer resources for cultural pursuits. From 499 BCE, when several cities in the region revolted from the Persian Empire, until the arrival of Alexander the Great in 334 BCE, western Anatolia was a battlefield. Battles were fought both on land and sea, and armies marched through the region regularly, commandeering local supplies and leaving the region impoverished. Not only Troy, but several of its neighbours also had little funds to spare for building works during this period.

Indeed, we know more about Classical Troy from literary sources and inscriptions than we do from archaeology. It is evident that the city was still inhabited, if only sparsely, and that it was still considered important for its cults as well as its Homeric past. Chief amongst these cults was that of Athena, which was housed in a temple on the summit of the citadel. Despite being the chief sanctuary of the city, this temple was described by Strabo as 'small and cheap' (Strabo, *Geography* 13.1.26), and nothing of it remains today. Nonetheless, we do know that the Trojans set up an honorific statue for the Persian satrap Ariobarzanes at the entrance to the precinct (Diodorus Siculus, *Library of History* 17.17.6), and that several notable figures stopped at the temple to offer sacrifices as they passed Troy on campaign. These included: the Persian king Xerxes, on his way to invade mainland Greece in 480 BCE (Herodotus, *The Histories* 7.43); the Spartan general Mindarus, before engaging the Athenian fleet on the Hellespont in 411 BCE (Xenophon, *Hellenica* 1.1.4); and, later, Alexander of Macedon himself (see Chapter 9).

From 499 to 449 BCE, the Persian Wars meant almost constant fighting between the Persian armies, and various allied Greek cities. A good deal of this fighting was carried out in western Anatolia, which also had to feed and support several armies on the move. Hosting Xerxes' army in 480 BCE, for example, would have been economically crippling. After the end of the Persian Wars, the cities of western Anatolia were subsumed under the imperial control of Athens, whose annual demands for tribute were scarcely less burdensome than those of their imperial predecessors, the Persians. Despite this, there is evidence for one new structure on the citadel of Troy from this time – a small building on the site of the later *bouleuterion*, or council chamber. The Peloponnesian War saw Spartan armies rampaging through the Troad once more, attacking Athenian strongholds. During the next two decades, the Troad passed from Spartan control back to the Persians, and then back again to the Spartans, before Troy was seized by a mercenary commander working for the Athenians (Demosthenes, *Against Aristocrates* 154; Aeneas Tacticus 24.5–8). The Athenian general Chares then seems to have controlled the Troad until Alexander arrived in 334 BCE.

Despite the rapid changes in government, some archaeological evidence suggests a gradual economic recovery in fourth-century Troy. The surviving deposits are, once more, ritual in nature, and come either from the Western Sanctuary or from the Temple of Athena. These include growing amounts of fineware pottery, much of it imported from Athens (presumably during the periods of Athenian ascendancy). This pottery seems to suggest ritual involving dining and drinking, and have been found alongside horse bones which show signs of having been prepared for food. Horse sacrifice would have been especially significant at Troy, with its legendary connection to Poseidon, the god of horses; the Trojan Horse; and the frequent mention in Homer of epic heroes sacrificing horses (e.g., *Iliad* 33.171ff). But while we know relatively little about the Classical city of Troy, we know much more about Troy's growing significance in the changing cultural world of the Classical period.

## Troy and the invention of the Greeks

The Trojan War became invested with a radical new meaning in the Classical period. In the wake of the Persian Wars, the old aristocratic associations of the Troy myth were transformed in the febrile political environment of democratic Athens.

For the first time, we find Trojans and Achaeans being portrayed differently in the iconography of Athenian painted vases. Whereas in previous periods, Trojans were usually depicted wearing the same clothes as Greeks, by the end of the fifth century Trojans were portrayed in an eastern, and specifically a Persian, fashion. In addition, the Trojan War was also now depicted alongside other mythic conflicts in a context that suggested civilizational struggle. For example, the metopes of the Parthenon featured the Trojan War on the north side; an Amazonomachy, or war between men and Amazons, on the west side; a Centauromachy, or war between men and Centaurs, on the south side; and a Gigantomachy, or war between the giants and the Olympian gods, on the east side. In each of these four cases, the struggle is one between the forces of order and civilization, and those of chaos and barbarity on the other. The Trojans are explicitly compared with the bestial giants, the subhuman centaur; and the dangerously transgressive female warriors, the Amazons. Trojans were portrayed in a similar context in the Stoa Poikile, or Painted Stoa, in the *agora* of Athens.[16]

The effect of all this was to distance the Trojans, culturally and ethnically, from the Greeks of the Classical age. Rather than models for aristocratic behaviour, Trojans were now examples of the quintessential Other – fundamentally different and opposite. They were elided with the contemporary Persians, and were given oriental and eastern traits. At the same time, they were compared with the mythical enemies of civilization, making them wholly alien and unsympathetic. After the Persian Wars, Greeks took a fresh look at the story of the Trojan War and saw it in a new light – as a clash of civilizations where an alliance of courageous European Greeks won a resounding victory over a despotic and degenerate Asian foe. Recent history was read back onto the mythical past, and the mythical past was reshaped in the image of recent history.

This shift is evident not only in the visual arts, but also in other forms of cultural expression. Tragic drama offers another good example. During the course of the fifth century, there was an increasing tendency to stereotype Trojans and other eastern groups, to elide them with Persians, and to characterize them as fundamentally different from Greeks. This process has sometimes been referred to as 'inventing the barbarian'. It is certainly true that before the Persian Wars, Greek ethnographic thinking recognized great cultural plurality. In contrast, after the Persian Wars there was a greater tendency to view all non-Greeks as essentially the same – as barbarians. The Persian Wars gave rise to a whole new way of thinking in the Greek world – Us and Them.[17]

As well as creating the concept of the barbarian, this process also led to the idea of the 'Greeks'. The idea of Greekness as an ethnicity, expressed through language and culture but essentially an innate and inborn quality, is the flip side of the invention of the barbarians. If Trojans were barbarians therefore, then the allied army of Achaeans and other groups who fought against them in the Trojan War must have been Greeks. It is to this period that we owe the idea of the Trojan War as being an ethnic and civilization conflict of Greeks against Trojans, Europe against Asia, West against East.

Herodotus, the 'Father of History', writing in Athens towards the end of the fifth century, ostensibly characterized the Trojan War in this way. In the prologue to his *Histories*, he lists a series of rapes where women were abducted from Europe to Asia and vice versa, culminating in the story of Helen and the Trojan War (Herodotus, *Histories* 1.1–4). From this point onwards, suggests Herodotus, there was an ancestral hatred between Europeans (for which read: Greeks) and Asians (for which read: Persians), which resulted in the Persian Wars, the main focus of his history. Under this perspective, the Trojan War was the spark that first ignited the clash of civilizations. Interestingly, Herodotus attributes this account of history to the Persians, rather than claiming it as his own view or that of his fellow Greeks. Indeed, Herodotus is at pains in the *Histories* to undermine the idea of a binary opposition between Us and Them, and many of his anecdotes actively celebrate cultural diversity.[18] His treatment of the Trojan War in the prologue seems to have been a conscious attempt to play to, or perhaps to play *with*, his Athenian audience.

The invention of a stark Greek–barbarian divide does seem to have been rooted firmly in Athens. The Persian Wars left Athens at the head of a coalition of disparate city states, which Athens quickly set about transforming into its empire. The idea of Greekness, and the call to band together in the face of a foreign enemy, was one of Athens' most powerful weapons in its ideological arsenal. It was vital, Athens argued, for the allies to remain under Athenian leadership as Persia still posed a threat. If persuasion did not work however, Athens was not above using more heavy-handed methods. In 416 BCE, for example, when Melos refused to sign up to the 'alliance', Athens slaughtered all the adult men of the island and sold the women and children into slavery (Thucydides, *History of the Peloponnesian War* 5.84-116).

The idea of Greeks as fundamentally different from, and ranged in opposition to, barbarians was therefore an ideological tool used by Athens to further its imperial ambitions. That is not to say that the idea did not catch on. Indeed, quite the opposite – it came to dominate much of the existing Greek literature, and has shaped the way we think about both the Greeks and the Trojan War today. The myth of Troy, like the contemporary world of the Classical Greeks, was increasingly painted in black and white rather than in technicolour.

## The on-site remains of Greek Troy

Very little can be seen today of Troy during the Greek period, partly due to problems of preservation, but mostly due to the poor and scanty nature of the remains themselves. Some trace of Archaic cult installations can sometimes be viewed in the area of the Western Sanctuary at Information Point 10, although this depends on the time of year and vegetation growth (Figure 8.1).

# Troy in the Hellenistic World, 334–85 BCE

The conquests of Alexander the Great ushered in a new era. For the first time, large portions of the Greek world were united under a single state with large portions of the non-Greek world. In Europe, this included the Aegean, Macedonia, and Thrace; in Africa, it incorporated Egypt and parts of Libya; and in Asia, it comprised Anatolia, the Levant, Mesopotamia, Persia, and central Asia as far as Bactria in modern-day Afghanistan.

Alexander's grand empire may have crumbled upon his death in 323 BCE, but his legacy of a broader Hellenistic world remained in place until Rome came to dominate some 200 years later. This Hellenistic world was made up of two large multiethnic empires, the Ptolemies based in Egypt and the Seleucids based in Mesopotamia, as well as a plethora of smaller states and kingdoms.[1] The kings of the Hellenistic world spent much of their time at war with each other, disputing territory and trade routes. Their people, by contrast, grew ever closer in terms of culture and society.

Alexander's conquests tied the various regions of the ancient world together, and encouraged a hitherto unimagined level of cultural interaction. Mixed marriages and multilingual families were common, with Greek culture and language acting as a common umbrella for all groups. A hybrid form of the Greek language emerged, known as *koine* Greek (literally: 'common Greek'), which became the standard language of literature and culture from Sicily to Samarkand.[2] Hybrid religious traditions also developed, which merged Greek gods with their Egyptian and Babylonian counterparts. Greek athletic practices became widely popular, and gymnasia became a standard feature of Hellenistic cities from Ai Khanoum on the Oxus to Ombi near the First Cataract of the Nile. This form of early globalization meant that the Hellenistic world was densely interconnected, with Greek culture as the common thread holding it together. To be Greek was no longer an ethnic claim as it had been in the Classical period, but rather a claim about culture and status.

At Troy, the Hellenistic remains constitute the final phases of the eighth level, Troy VIII. During this period Troy once more began to expand, drawing its importance, as ever, from its glorious mythic heritage. Troy during this period also enjoyed the direct patronage of several Hellenistic rulers, the most important and famous of whom was Alexander of Macedon himself.

## Alexander at Troy (334 BCE)

Alexander arrived in the Troad in 334 BCE, with a fearsome army of Macedonian warriors at his back. He fought the first of his three major pitched battles against the Persians here, near the River Granicus just to the east of Troy.[3] Alexander was victorious, crushing the combined army of the western Persian satraps with a single blow, and clearing the way for his march through Anatolia.

On his way to the Granicus, Alexander stopped at Troy (Arrian, *Anabasis* 1.11.5–8; Strabo, *Geography* 13.1.26; Diodorus Siculus, *Library of History* 17.18; Plutarch, *Life of Alexander* 15). As we have seen in Chapter 8, Troy at this time was relatively small and poor, although it still had considerable cultural cachet. Alexander's actions at Troy seem to have been calculated to make the most of this cultural capital, and to turn the myth of the Trojan War to his own advantage.[4] Indeed, he signalled his interest in the myth even before he reached the Troad. At Elaious, on the northern shore of the Hellespont almost directly across the straits from Troy, Alexander stopped at the tomb of Protesilaus and made sacrifices to the dead hero.

Protesilaus was supposedly the first man to jump ashore when the Achaean fleet landed at Troy (Pausanias, *Description of Greece* 4.2.7), and also the first man to die in the conflict (Apollodorus, *Epitome* 3.29). He later received honours and a cult at Elaious, where it was claimed that he was buried. During the Achaemenid period, a Persian satrap called Artayctes had reportedly desecrated Protesilaus' tomb, stealing the treasures that had been dedicated there, giving over the lands for agriculture, and using the sanctuary for his amorous liaisons (Herodotus, *Histories* 9.116). The excuse Artayctes had given for this sacrilege was that Protesilaus had spearheaded an impious invasion of Asia, and therefore deserved the desecration. In Chapter 8, it was mentioned that the Persian King, Xerxes, reportedly visited Troy, supposedly aligning himself with the ancient Trojans as a rhetorical justification for his own campaign against the Greeks. It seems that Artayctes may have done something similar with Protesilaus' tomb. In this context, Alexander's visit to the tomb was not a matter of personal piety or even of cultural tourism. It was a political act, setting Alexander and his Macedonian army up as the heirs of the Homeric Achaeans, avenging the outrages committed by the Persian heirs of the Homeric Trojans.

At Troy itself, Alexander made sacrifices to the goddess Athena and the heroes of the Trojan War. He also visited the tomb of Achilles, which he honoured with garlands and libations, as well as staging a running race around the burial mound. Meanwhile, his companion Hephaistion gave similar honours to the tomb of Patroclus. These actions suggest that the young general had a flair for the dramatic. But Alexander also sought to help Troy with a series of practical measures. Once the Battle of the Granicus was won, he returned to Troy and put in place a practical programme of rebuilding and civic improvement: rebuilding the Temple of Athena, exempting the city from taxation, and establishing sacred games in honour of Athena (Strabo, *Geography* 13.1.26). Although Alexander's untimely death prevented him from fulfilling these promises, some of these plans were eventually carried out by his successors.

Why did Alexander bother with Troy? Like others before and after him, Alexander was drawn here not by the city of Troy but by its story. Following the new interpretations of the story found in the Classical period (see Chapter 8), the Trojan War offered Alexander a model and a metaphor – it set a mythic pattern for conflict between east and west, Asia and Europe, Greek and barbarian. Given Alexander's grand aim to conquer the Persian Empire and to rule all of Asia as well as Greece, it is easy to see the political expediency of embracing this interpretation and of drawing parallels between his own campaign and the Trojan War story.

For Alexander however, the political was also personal. Casting himself as the new Achilles was more than mere posturing. His family on his mother's side had long claimed to be descended in a direct line from Achilles, and there are signs that Alexander may have been personally invested in the Trojan War myth. It is said that he brought a copy of the *Iliad* with him wherever he travelled, sleeping with it under his pillow at night (Plutarch, *Life of Alexander* 8). Like many before and after him, Alexander was mesmerised by the tale of Troy.

## Rebuilding and renewal

After the death of Alexander, the Troad came under the control of two of Alexander's generals in quick succession – Antigonus (known as 'Monophthalmus', literally the 'one-eyed') and Lysimachus. These men sought to keep the promises made by Alexander to the Trojans, and rebuilding at the city began in grand style (Figure 9.1).[5]

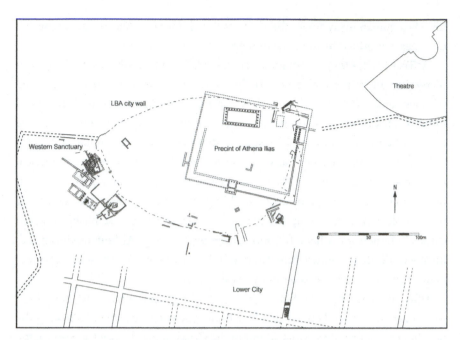

**Figure 9.1** Plan of Troy during the Hellenistic period.

The *agora*, or central marketplace, was one of the first areas to undergo extensive redevelopment. This lay on the plain, just to the southeast of the mound and right under the still-towering remains of the Troy VI citadel walls. A new *bouleuterion* (council chamber) was built with dramatic views onto the ancient fortifications. A large theatre was also built to the northeast of the citadel mound. Designed to hold audiences of up to 10,000 people, the theatre is evidence, perhaps not so much for an expanded population, but certainly for the city's power to attract visitors on a grand scale.

Although many of these visitors would have been drawn to Troy by its mythic heritage, in this period there was also a new and more practical reason coming to the city. A new league, or *koinon*, was created which bound many cities of the Troad into a kind of cultic and political alliance. This league was focused on the Temple of Athena at Troy, which hosted both the league meetings and its annual religious festival. The city benefitted greatly from the regular influx of people and funds, and this growing prosperity is obvious in its material culture. Around 300 BCE, the city began to mint coins for the first time, featuring images of its patron goddess Athena on both sides of the new coinage (Figure 9.2).

The city continued to prosper under the control of the Seleucid kings, who took control of the Troad in 281 BCE.[6] The Seleucids offered their patronage, and in return received honours in the form of statues and altars set up in their name, as well as the renaming of a month 'Seleukios' (at this stage, individual cities still determined their own calendars). Inscriptions from this time detail the institution of new festivals and sanctuaries, including a *Baseileion* (a sanctuary of kings) and a cult of Zeus Polieus (literally, 'Zeus of the city').

A massive new building programme was instituted in the 230s, under the Seleucid usurper Antiochus Hierax. The lower city, now occupied again, was reorganized on a grid plan and surrounded by a stone fortification wall. The area inside the fortifications was considerable – about 72 hectares. Not all of this area was densely occupied, as it included the theatre and cultivated horticultural zones as well as domestic and industrial areas. In their work, the Hellenistic builders sought to equal and improve on the last era of Trojan brilliance. Where it touched the citadel, the new wall partly made use of and partly demolished the previous Late Bronze Age fortifications; and in its circuit of the lower city, it incorporated the Late Bronze Age defensive ditch.

The Western Sanctuary continued as an area for cult and ritual.[7] A series of medium-sized temples were constructed here, and the open-air altars in the Upper and Lower Sanctuaries were modified and expanded. Judging from the votive figurines, two main cults were located here – that of the hero Dardanus, the mythical ancestor of the Trojans; and that of Cybele, a Anatolian mother goddess whose worship spread across the Mediterranean in the Classical and Hellenistic periods.[8]

In the wider Troad, other cities were also expanding and rebuilding around this time, as well as aligning themselves with Troy through the new league. Immediately around Troy, the antiquarian interest in monuments of the Trojan War found a new outlet in the 'heroic burials' that dotted the landscape. These were usually prehistoric mounds, which over the centuries had attracted stories that linked them to Trojan War legend. Most of them were identified as the burial sites of important Homeric heroes, including Achilles, Patroclus, Hector, Ajax, and Hecuba. One good example is the mound of Sivritepe, now usually assumed to have been the 'tomb of Achilles'. This mound was enlarged and monumentalized in the mid-third century, so that it was taller and more impressive.[9] Projects such as this were clearly designed to capitalize on the Iliadic heritage, and would have had the dual benefits of promoting tourism and symbolically strengthening Troy's hold over its territory and allies in the league.

The Seleucid patronage declined over the course of the third century as the Troad came under the influence of a new power – the Attalid dynasty based in Pergamon, backed by their allies the Romans. When these formidable powers consolidated their control of the region in the early second century, they treated Troy kindly and granted the city exemption from taxes once more. This special status was conceded because the Romans claimed descent from the refugees who fled at the end of the Trojan War, and so looked to contemporary Troy as their mother-city (see Chapter 10). From this point onwards, Roman interests became a crucial point of reference for Troy.

## The Temple of Athena

Perhaps the most impressive construction of the Hellenistic period was the new Temple of Athena. This was a large-scale project which seems to have been started during the rebuilding programme of the 230s BCE, but which took over eighty years to complete. For the first time, the temple was truly monumental, measuring 16.4 × 35.7 m, and made entirely from marble. This huge new building stood within a massive open sanctuary, which measured 109 × 88 m and occupied more than half the space on the citadel mound (Figure 9.1).

In order to create such a large flat space, the Hellenistic builders had to create a huge terrace upon which the sanctuary could sit. This involved shaving off the top of the curved hill, destroying much of the Bronze and Iron Age remains, as well as the Greek levels in the process. It also involved building enormous terrace walls to hold up the edges of the precinct. The Hellenistic builders made use of

**Figure 9.2** Coin struck by Ilion in the second century BCE, depicting the head of Athena on the obverse and the cult image of Athena Ilias on the reverse.

the Bronze Age city walls to help with this work, and the northeast corner of the sanctuary rests upon the Northeast Bastion of Troy VI. The entire complex could only be entered through a monumental gateway, or Propylaea. The road to the Propylaea led up from the agora on the plain, passing through the still-standing remains of the Troy VI fortification walls in the original location of the Bronze Age South Gate. Here, as was often the case at Troy, the heroic past was still very much a part of the city's historical present.

This is also true of a mysterious feature found within the precinct. It is a small circular structure built of marble, under which was a deep well which could only be accessed through a long underground passage. It is not completely clear what the function of this strange monument would have been, although it has been suggested that it may have been connected to the ritual of the Locrian Maidens. This ritual recalled how Ajax of Locris (a different character from the main Ajax, who came from Salamis) raped Cassandra during the fall of Troy, and apparently involved aristocratic girls from Locris being sent to Troy as a form of tribute to atone for Ajax's crime.[10] If this is indeed the case, then this is yet another case of the Iliadic heritage of the city being featured in its civic landscape.

This was also true of the temple itself. Built in the Doric order, the temple featured sculpted metopes, which are only partially preserved.[11] On the north side, these metopes depicted the myth of the Trojan War. Scenes include the death of Sarpedon; fierce conflict involving people dressed in typical 'eastern' fashion; and the god Apollo riding on his chariot, perhaps cursing the Achaeans with the plague that we find in *Iliad* Book 1 (Figure 9.3). The choice of location is important. The north was a long side of the temple, the farthest from the main precinct gateway and not immediately visible to a visitor entering the sanctuary. The north metopes did, however, overlook the edge of the citadel mound, facing out to hinterland and the Hellespont beyond. Anyone looking up from the open countryside to the north of the city would therefore have had an unobstructed view of the Trojan War metopes, which were brightly painted to make them more easily visible at a distance.

The temple metopes did more than simply evoke the city's mythic past. The three other sides of the temple featured a Gigantomachy, an Amazonomachy, and a Centauromachy (for definitions of these terms, see Chapter 8). Although these subjects have little direct relevance to the city of Troy, this decorative scheme was already well known by the Hellenistic period. It adorned the metopes of yet another even more famous Temple of Athena – the Parthenon of Athens, built in the Classical period. The Trojan Temple of Athena features exactly the same sculptural themes as the Athenian Parthenon, in exactly the same order.

Why did the Trojans of the Hellenistic period seek to replicate the sculptural scheme of a famous temple in Athens? Interestingly, the temple metopes were not the only place where Hellenistic Troy set out to reference Classical Athens. As mentioned above, Troy staged an annual festival of Athena to bring together the members of the Troad league. This festival was known as the Panathenaea – the same name given to Athens' annual festival in honour of the goddess. And Troy, like Athens, held a grander version of the festival once every four years, during which they sponsored athletic, poetic, and musical competitions.[12] Troy's coins during this period are also suspiciously Athenian looking – on one side featuring what must have been the cult image of Athena and, on the other, depicting the helmeted head of Athena in a similar fashion as on Classical Athenian coins.

It is not clear why Troy should have modelled its cult of Athena on that of Athens. Athens was no longer the dominant political power in the region, nor was it the main cultural capital of the Greek world. In the Hellenistic period, cities such as Alexandria, Babylon, and Pergamon fulfilled this latter role. It is possible that Troy's interest in the symbols of Classical Athens had more to do with internal dynamics within western Anatolia than with Athens itself. Around the same time, several cities in the region all chose to 'buy into' Athenian traditions, creating something of a fashion for Athenian styles and practices from a few generations earlier. Perhaps there was an element of keeping up with the neighbours in Troy's engagement with the Athenian past.

## Troy and the scholars

After the death of Alexander, the Classical idea of the Trojan War as a clash of civilizations became less appealing. In the multicultural world of the Hellenistic period, a new understanding of Troy was needed. What had been a politicized myth in the Classical period now became intellectualized, taken over by scholars and subsumed into a new kind of elite high culture.

As already mentioned, Greekness in the Hellenistic period was not an issue of ethnicity, but of engagement with Greek culture. This was necessarily linked to class, as elites and rulers across the Near East were usually the descendants of Alexander's Macedonian generals. In the courts of the Hellenistic kings, therefore, knowledge was power. These kings sponsored the building of great libraries and maintained thriving communities of scholars, housing them at international

**Figure 9.3** The Helios metope from the Hellenistic Temple of Athena at Troy.

centres of learning such as the library at Pergamon and the famous library of Alexandria.[13]

Poets competed with each other to demonstrate their erudition and knowledge of Greek legend, and to include evermore obscure mythic details into their work.[14] Many of these poets were also textual scholars, including the prolific Callimachus, who wrote hymns, elegies and epigrams as well as the *Aitia* (literally, 'Causes'), a lengthy poem recounting myths which lay behind unusual rituals or cult practices. His colleague, Apollonius Rhodius, wrote a series of poems recounting the foundation of notable cities, as well as the *Argonautica* – an epic about Jason and the Argonauts. Another author, the mysterious Lycophron, penned the *Alexandra* – a long poem, ostensibly narrated by the Trojan prophet Cassandra, which touched on an encyclopaedic array of mythic episodes through riddling and obscure references.

In this context, the story of the Trojan War became evermore closely associated with Homer and the *Iliad*. The epic became a source of scholarly debate and bookish dispute, with the librarians at Alexandria pouring over different manuscripts of the texts, offering their comments and emendations. Indeed, many of the Homeric *scholia* date to this period – ancient commentaries on the text which contain vital information for understanding the poems and wider Greek myth. It is during this period that the *Iliad* was divided into twenty-four books and that accents and punctuation were added.

In keeping with this erudite interest in the obscure details of the Troy story, some of the best-known works of Hellenistic art take as their subject, not the main characters and heroes of the myth, but the lesser-known figures. The Trojan priest Laocoön is one such figure (Figure 9.4). According to myth, Laocoön tried to warn the Trojans not to bring the Wooden Horse into the city, but was dragged into the sea, along with his sons, by serpents. The famous statue of Laocoön known today is a Roman copy of a Hellenistic original, executed in the vibrant and dynamic style of the Pergamene School. It is unclear exactly what the Hellenistic original may have looked like – the Roman sculptors likely

**Figure 9.4** Copy of a Hellenistic statue of Laocoön and his sons.

innovated on the design, and the surviving statue today has undergone many restorations from the renaissance to the present day.[15]

## The Trojan War, epic origins, and the start of history

We have already seen in Chapter 8 how many Greek cities traced their origins to the fallout of the Trojan War. Specifically, the Achaean heroes returning from Troy were said to have founded these cities while on their long and tortuous journeys home. In the Hellenistic period, this idea of the Trojan War being a fount of origins spread, and interest in foundation myths rooted in Homeric epic skyrocketed.

Works focusing on local history, poems recounting origin myths (known as *ktisis* poems), and heroic genealogies became more popular in the Hellenistic period than ever before. The Macedonian kings and dynasts were foremost amongst those seeking to claim an illustrious ancient past – in the Classical period, Macedonians were not usually considered to be Greeks, and they were often therefore at pains to establish a Hellenic genealogy.[16] Many cities were also new at this time, and these were often keen to acquire for themselves some connection to mythic antiquity. Even those cities which were long established showed a renewed interest in their past, as they sought to make sense of their place in the changing world order.

Some authors sought to trace not just the origins of dynasties and cities back to the Trojan War, but the beginning of recordable time itself. Already in the Classical period, the historians Herodotus and Thucydides had classified the Trojan War as belonging to mythic rather than historical time (Herodotus, *Histories* 1.3–5; Thucydides, *The Peloponnesian War* 1.9-12). In the Hellenistic period, attempts were now made to quantify this scientifically.

The geographer and natural scientist Eratosthenes produced one of the first chronographical works – designing a dating system and assigning precise years to past historical events. He began his work with the Trojan War, claiming that it could be dated to 1184/3 BCE. When Apollodorus wrote his *Chronica* a century later, he also started history with the Trojan War. From here on, the fall of Troy became the established cut-off point between myth and history, between the heroic world of legend and the baser age of human frailty. The very concept of time was divided into period – before and after 'the fall'.

## The Fimbrian sack of Troy (85 BCE)

The Hellenistic city of Troy, like so many of its precursors, ended abruptly with a destruction in 85 BCE. Unlike earlier destructions, we have good documentary evidence for this happening as the result of a siege. The man responsible for this siege of Troy was no Homeric Agamemnon however, but a renegade Roman commander, Gaius Flavius Fimbria.

By this time, Troy was part of the new Roman province of Asia, which spanned much of western and central Anatolia. Rome had acquired its new imperial possessions (almost) bloodlessly, when the last Attalid king of Pergamon died in 133 BCE and bequeathed his kingdom to his long-time ally, Rome. The quarrelsome Fimbria had originally been sent to Asia Minor to serve under the general Valerius Flaccus, but he quickly argued with his boss and found an opportunity to stir up a revolt against him. Killing the governor, Fimbria turned his attention to a coalition of cities that had rebelled against Rome, led by Mithridates the King of Pontus in the First Mithridatic War. When he came to Troy, the Trojans barred their walls against him, and Fimbria then laid siege to the city, capturing it after only eleven days. He is said to have done terrible things in the city and caused much destruction (Strabo, *Geography* 13.1.27; Appian, *Roman History* 12.53; Augustine, *On the City of God* 3.7).

The archaeology does indeed show clear evidence for violence around this time.[17] Several of the cult buildings in the Western Sanctuary were burned, although the buildings had been emptied of their contents and cleaned before the burning happened. It seems that the occupants of the city knew that Fimbria was coming, and had enough time to bring all precious items inside the citadel walls.

## The remains of Hellenistic Troy

The remains of Hellenistic Troy can be viewed today in two places. The first is the Western Sanctuary area, at Information Point 10. The specifically Hellenistic elements are limited to parts of the Upper Sanctuary, which include the following: the northeastern stretch of the sanctuary's wall, the well-dressed masonry clearly following the line of the Troy VI fortification wall directly behind it; and the rectangular base of the open-air altar that once stood at the centre of the Upper Sanctuary (marked No. 3 on the information panel).

Parts of the Hellenistic Temple of Athena are also still visible at Information Point 3. From this vantage point, standing on top of the Troy VI Northeast Bastion, the visitor is roughly at the same height as the ground level of the Hellenistic temple terrace. Many of the fragments of masonry along the path between here and Information Point 4 are parts of marble decoration of the Temple of Athena, including a chunk of the coffered ceiling of the temple's interior. Other fragments from the Hellenistic temple can be seen strewn around the site. The sculpted metopes from the temple are on display at the Pergamon Museum in Berlin, where they were donated by Schliemann upon his death.

# Troy in the Roman World, 85 BCE to Seventh Century

The expanding empire of Rome looked to Troy for its mythical roots – the Romans claimed descent from Aeneas, one of the lesser royals of Troy, who fled after the sack of the city. This guaranteed Troy a privileged position within the Empire, a position that the Trojans seem to have been only too happy to accept.

The first few decades of direct Roman rule did not bring immediate benefits to the city. The Romans were still in the process of consolidating their power in the eastern Mediterranean, meeting resistance and rebellion along the way. There was also considerable instability at Rome itself in the first century BCE. The old system of the Republic became increasingly dysfunctional, as a small group of leading generals began to seize and dispute power amongst themselves.[1] The names of these generals resonate even today: Sulla, who marched his armies against Rome in 84 BCE, only one year after the Fimbrian sack of Troy, and assumed the title of *dictator*; Crassus, famed for his incredible wealth; Pompey, awarded the title *Magnus* for his victories against Rome's enemies in the east; and, of course, Julius Caesar, who claimed the title of *imperator* and whose regime marked the final nail in the coffin of the Roman Republic.

Throughout this turbulent century, Troy remained impoverished, as did most of the cities of Asia Minor.[2] An inscription from the city records additional soldiers assigned to protect it from the raids of Cilician pirates, while another documents the Trojans' gratitude to Pompey for his direct assistance against these pirates. The Troad league was also in trouble – Troy's local allies could no longer make their annual payments into the league coffers to fund the Panathenaea festival, and inscriptions have been found drawing up complex loan agreements. Indeed, when Julius Caesar visited the city in 48 BCE, he apparently found it lying mostly in ruins. The poet Lucan describes Caesar seeking out the great walls of myth and describes how trees had grown over the place where the ancient palaces had once stood (Lucan, *Pharsalia* 9.964–77, 999).[3] Caesar seems to have hoped to reverse the decline, allotting more territory to Troy and confirming its tax-free status (Strabo, *Geography* 13.1.27).

It was not until Augustus replaced the Republic with the Principate in 27 BCE and established the Julio-Claudian dynasty of emperors that things really began to change. At this point, Troy enjoyed something of a renaissance. The traces of this are evident everywhere in the archaeological record. The remains of Troy IX – the last of the nine cities of Troy – demonstrate the wealth and prosperity of Troy in the Roman world.

## A Trojan renaissance

A number of major new construction projects were undertaken in Troy IX (Figure 10.1). Most of these were located around the base of the mound or in the lower city, as the Hellenistic Sanctuary of Athena still dominated the top of the mound.[4]

The Western Sanctuary continued in use as a cult area, although it was dramatically remodelled. The temples that had been burnt during the Fimbrian sack were not rebuilt, and many of their stones were taken and reused in new structures elsewhere. The ground level was raised to cover most of the earlier remains, using soil excavated from the southwestern side of the mound directly behind the sanctuary area. A *stoa* (a covered portico) was constructed in this newly levelled area during the reign of the emperor Augustus, overlooking the Western Sanctuary.

It was not until the final quarter of the first century CE, however, that a new building programme was initiated in the Western Sanctuary area itself. An open-air altar was built at the new higher ground level, and one of the earlier temples was renovated. Finally, a podium was constructed which seems to have served as a grandstand for viewing ceremonies and other performances. This grandstand would have provided seating for up to 360 people, suggesting that the events staged here would have been relatively popular. The nature of these performances or rituals remains mysterious, as does the recipients of the cult practiced here. Figurines of Cybele and the horseman plaques of Dardanus were no longer deposited in the area, and there are signs that their worship may have moved out further into the lower city (see below).

The new Augustan *stoa* overlooking the Western Sanctuary was one of a pair, with the other running along the southern edge of the mound, parallel with the precinct wall of the Athena sanctuary and overlooking the *agora*. Yet another *stoa* was built during the reign of Claudius, the physical remains of which are now almost completely lost but for which we still have the dedicatory

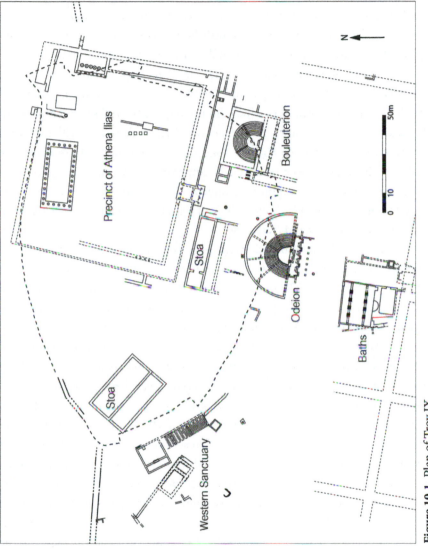

**Figure 10.1** Plan of Troy IX.

inscription. This *stoa* seems to have provided a grand setting for the display of statues of the imperial family.

The *agora* itself was revamped in spectacular style. Troy's first Roman-style baths were built on its west side, probably on the site of the Hellenistic gymnasium. The baths feature mosaics of athletes and warriors engaging in combat, and are a sign that the Trojans were beginning to embrace the new customs and social norms that came with Rome. The baths were extended and refurbished by the emperor Hadrian in the early second century CE.

Hadrian also attached an *odeion* to the baths. This was a small theatre, seating between 1,700 and 2,100 people, and would have been used for meetings and smaller musical performances which did not require the full seating capacity of the main theatre (see below). The *odeion* was lavishly decorated with expensive and rare coloured marbles, and the stage area was adorned with over-life-size sculptures including one representing the emperor Hadrian himself (Figure 10.2). Later during the second century, a temple to the nymphs (or *nymphaeum*) was added to the bath complex, built entirely of marble and including water features and statues of nymphs and river gods.

Troy's main theatre also underwent large-scale renovation, probably in the final stages of the first century CE, around the same time as the rebuilding in the Western Sanctuary. The stage and its *skene* (backdrop) were rebuilt in grand fashion and adorned with impressive life-size sculptures, and the seating area was reorganized according to administrative subdivisions of the citizen body.

The lower city of Troy IX was increasingly densely occupied. There does not seem to have been much in the way of spatial separation between commercial and domestic premises, and household industries seem to have been carried out in many homes. The buildings were organized on a grid plan in blocks, or *insulae*. The plan as a whole was centred on a main street running north-south, which led directly to the main entrance to the citadel. It seems that some cult activities were carried out here in the lower city – Cybele figurines and the characteristic horseman plaques associated with the hero Dardanus have been found here. These terracottas may have been manufactured at Troy itself – a ceramics workshop has been uncovered in the lower city, which used moulds to mass-produce figurines and incense burners.

The population of the city seems to have expanded gradually throughout the Roman period, and by the late second century CE a second bath complex was built on the eastern edge of the town. By the mid-third century, occupation in the lower city was so dense that new buildings had to be squeezed in the spaces between existing structures, rather than being freestanding. Around this time, it seems that industrial activities were moved outside the main residential zone, with workshops located out to the east of the theatre.

**Figure 10.2** Statue of Hadrian found beneath the Troy IX *Odeion*.

## The Julio-Claudians in Troy (27 BCE–68 CE)

The first emperor of Rome, Augustus, established the dynasty of the Julio-Claudians in 27 BCE. While all Romans were supposedly descended from Troy, the Julio-Claudian family in particular claimed their own privileged Trojan ancestry. They traced their family back through the generations to the leader of the Trojans in Italy, Aeneas, who was the son of Anchises, one of Priam's cousins, and the goddess Aphrodite. Julius Caesar's visit to Troy was not just a stop on the regular tourist route, but a return to the ancestral homeland. It was even rumoured that Caesar had planned to move the capital of the Empire from Rome back to Troy (Suetonius, *Divus Julius* 79; Nicolaus of Damascus, *Life of Augustus* 20.68).

Caesar's adopted son, Augustus, was to follow in his footsteps. Augustus visited the city in 20 BCE, kick-starting the first of several phases of intense rebuilding during the Roman period.[5] The two *stoas* on the southern and southwestern edge of the mound likely owe to his patronage, for which the Trojans awarded him unparalleled civic honours. Statues of Augustus and other members of the imperial family have been found dotted around the city, as well as inscriptions marking the dedication of altars or precincts to them. Indeed, a dedication to Augustus appears in the Temple of Athena itself.

Other members of the Julio-Claudian family also made a point of visiting Troy. Augustus' daughter Julia travelled to see Troy, as did her husband, the general Agrippa, sometime between 16 and 13 BCE. Julia's visit started out badly, however. The local river of the Scamander was in flood, and she was nearly swept away by the torrent. Although Julia escaped safely, Agrippa was furious with the Trojans for not doing more to help her (Nicolaus of Damascus, Fragment 134; Josephus, *Antiquities of the Jews* 16.16).

Some years later in 18 CE, the young general Germanicus also visited the city (Tacitus, *Annals* 2.54). He may have been accompanied by his wife, Agrippina the Elder, as a statue head depicting her has been found on the site. Germanicus' mother, Antonia the Younger, may also have come to Troy, as an inscription has been found which records her donation of funds to cover the costs of local magistrates. In this inscription, she is flattered with a comparison to the goddess Aphrodite, and is explicitly said to be 'of the race of Anchises'.

## Troy in Julio-Claudian Rome

As well as offering their patronage to the city of Troy, the Julio-Claudians also celebrated their Trojan ancestry back at home in Rome. The story of how their ancestor, Aeneas, fled the fall of Troy and settled in Italy featured strongly in the imperial discourse. The actual founding of the city of Rome may have been traditionally attributed to Romulus, but under the Julio-Claudians, Aeneas' arrival in Latium came to be viewed as an essential part of Rome's foundation myth. In the iconography and rhetoric of the Augustan age in particular, it is Aeneas rather than Romulus who features most often in representations of Roman origins.[6]

The story of how the Trojans became Romans is perhaps most famously told in Virgil's epic poem, the *Aeneid*, which was written under the direct patronage of Augustus. The entire work was designed to extol the greatness of Rome and of its new ruling dynasty, the Julio-Claudians. Nowhere is this more evident than in Book 6, where Aeneas visits the underworld. Here, he meets the souls of men who are waiting to be born, including those of his future descendants. These include not only the legendary kings of Rome and famous heroes of the Republic, but also key Julio-Claudians. Julius Caesar and Augustus are described in particularly glowing terms. When surveying the future souls, Aeneas is told to:

> look upon this race of your Romans:
> Here is Caesar and all the descendants of the Iulus who will pass beneath the heavens.
> And here is the man, here he is, who you have often heard prophecies about,
> Augustus Caesar, descended from Jove

Virgil, *Aeneid* 6.788–792

Also writing around this time was the historian Livy, who treated the same material in Book 1 of his massive history of Rome, *Ab Urbe Condita* (literally, 'From the Foundation of the City'). Indeed, it is significant that Livy chose to begin his history of Rome with '*Troia capta*' – the sack of Troy (Livy, *From the Foundation of the City* 1.1).

The story also featured heavily in the visual arts of the time. In particular, the image of Aeneas fleeing Troy, carrying his father Anchises on his back while clasping the hand of his son Ascanius, was instantly recognizable. The original prototype for this image was the statue group set up in the Forum of Augustus sometime between 17 and 5 BCE (Figure 10.3). This statue group stood in prime position, directly opposite the statue of Romulus. The image was reproduced widely throughout the Roman world in a range of different media, from terracotta figures to wall paintings.[7]

The story of Aeneas' flight from Troy and arrival in Italy was everywhere in the Rome of the Julio-Claudians. The myth of the Trojan War had therefore been fundamentally reinterpreted – it was less significant for the war itself, as for the aftermath of the war. The fall of Troy was reimagined as the birth of Rome.

**Figure 10.3** Reconstruction of the statue group of Aeneas, Anchises, and Ascanius in the Forum Augustum.

And this reimagining of the myth was fundamentally connected to the discourse of political power, and to the ruling Julio-Claudian dynasty. The mad emperor Nero reportedly sang about the fall of Troy while Rome burned (Tacitus, *Annals* 15.39.3). It is also said that Germanicus penned a short poem when he visited Troy, which illustrates the deeply political role the city had within the Roman world at this time.

> Hector of the blood of Ares, if you hear me wherever you are beneath the ground,
> Greetings! Let you sighs for your homeland be but small.
> Ilion is inhabited – a famous city. It holds men who are feebler
> Than you, but who are still lovers of war.
> The Myrmidons have been erased. Stand next to Achilles
> And tell him that all Thessaly is subject to the sons of Aeneas.
>
> *Greek Anthology*, 9.387

## Troy until and under Hadrian (68–138 CE)

The reign of Nero, the last of the Julio-Claudians, fell apart with rebellions and revolts in 68 CE. The dynasty that eventually emerged from the chaos a year later was the Flavians, the first emperor of which was the veteran general Vespasian. The Flavians did not have the same ancestral links to Aeneas as the Julio-Claudians, and they did not engage in promoting the specific myth of Aeneas in the same way as their immediate predecessors had done.

On a more general level, the connection with Troy as the mother-city of Rome remained strong, and the Flavians continued to show the city imperial favour. The city flourished. The refurbishment of the theatre probably dates from around this time, as does the renovation of the Western Sanctuary. It seems that the Trojans now began to realize the potential benefits of their Roman connections. It was around this time that Troy began to mint coins depicting the canonical image of Aeneas fleeing Troy (Figure 10.4), although in Rome coins had featured this image since the time of Julius Caesar.

The next major chapter in the development of the city came with the reign of Emperor Hadrian. Around the turn of the century, a series of earthquakes had left the city in need of some repair, and Hadrian proved himself more than equal to the challenge. He visited Troy in 124 CE, during his tour of the province of Asia. A significant revival is associated with Hadrian's visit. He seems to have sponsored the building of the *odeion*, the expansion of the bath complex, and the new aqueduct that was constructed to ensure a clean water supply for the city. The latter proved to be fantastically expensive, and once the emperor's grant for the works had been spent, the governor of Asia had to pay for the remaining costs out of his own pocket.[8]

Hadrian also paid for a full-scale rebuilding of the Tomb of Ajax, which lay to the north of the city. As we saw in Chapter 8, the presence of several large tumulus mounds in the immediate vicinity of Troy led to these being identified with the burials of prominent Homeric heroes. It seems that the mound associated with Ajax was, in particular, badly in need of repair, and so Hadrian ordered the construction of an entirely new mound (Philostratus, *Heroicus* 8.1).[9]

Hadrian's interest in Troy was subtly different from that of the Julio-Claudians. Where previous Roman emperors honoured the ancient Trojan past, and commemorated the fall of Troy as the precursor of the foundation of Rome, Hadrian did something new. He explicitly celebrated the Greek as well as the Trojan aspects of the Trojan War myth. Whereas the Julio-Claudian Germanicus chose to frame his visit in terms of ongoing rivalries between Trojans/Romans and Achaeans/Greeks, Hadrian is best known for his restoration of the Tomb of Ajax – an Achaean, rather than a Trojan, hero. It is hard to imagine a Julio-Claudian emperor doing something similar. Hadrian's choice must have been partly informed by his wider outlook. He had a reputation for being a philhellene, and bestowed significant patronage over the Greek cities of the east during his reign.[10]

**Figure 10.4** Reverse face of a coin minted by Ilion, depicting Aeneas, leading his son Ascanius and carrying his father Anchises.

## Troy under Caracalla and the later emperors (138–262 CE)

In the period after Hadrian, many of the cities of Asia Minor enjoyed imperial patronage, prosperity, and a construction boom. This does not seem to have been the case for Troy, and the only new building here during the Antonine period was the temple to the nymphs (the *nymphaeum*) appended to the bath complex in the forum. It was not until the Severan dynasty took power that the city's fortunes once more began to look up.

The emperor Caracalla visited Troy in 214 CE, an event that was commemorated by the city with the issuing of a special coin featuring a portrait of the emperor (Cassius Dio, *Roman History* 77.16.7; Herodian, *History of the Empire* 4.8.2–3). Caracalla seems to have responded by bestowing his imperial favour on the city, starting work on the rebuilding of the *odeion* and giving the city grants of money.

Caracalla followed Hadrian in focusing on the Achaean rather than the Trojan heroes of the Trojan War. He set up a new statue of Achilles, which seems to have been larger than life-size, and placed it in direct opposition of a smaller statue of Hector.[11] He also paid particular attention to the tomb of

Achilles, honouring the hero with sacrifices and races around the tomb. With these actions, Caracalla styled himself as a new Alexander. Given that Caracalla was passing through Troy on his way to fight the eastern empire of the Parthians, it is perhaps unsurprising that he would want to draw parallels between himself and Alexander, who had also passed by this way on his way to fight the eastern empire of the Persians more than five centuries before.

One of the stranger things that Caracalla did was to build a completely new tumulus mound for his favourite freedman, Festus. Festus died at Troy, and Caracalla took the opportunity to stage a lavish burial for him that explicitly recalled the Homeric burial of Patroclus. Festus, then, was cast as the Patroclus to Caracalla's Achilles: just as Alexander had cast his own companion, Hephaistion, as Patroclus to his own Achilles. Festus' burial mound still stands today as the tallest of all the tumuli in the Troad, and is known as Üveciktepe.

## The Gothic sack of Troy and beyond

Troy was sacked once more, in 262 CE, by a band of Goths who also raided a number of other cities in Asia Minor.[12] We are told that Troy at the time was little more than a ruin and still recovering from its sack by Agamemnon, and that the Goths destroyed what little had been rebuilt (Jordanus, *Getica* 20.108). This description of Troy's poverty is clearly exaggerated, but it is possible that the Goths did arrive to find a city already partially destroyed. A number of earthquakes happened around this time, and it seems that they had a major impact on the city. Therefore, while there is plenty of archaeological evidence for destructions at Troy, it is impossible to tell what damage might have been done by the Goths, and what by natural disasters.

Who or whatever was responsible, Troy never recovered from these destructions, and the city suffered a long, slow decline lasting several centuries. Even the personal visits of two further emperors, Constantine and Julian, could not turn this tide. Constantine apparently considered building a palace at Troy and making it his capital city in the early fourth century. It is said that he got as far as building some city walls before he gave up on the site and relocated to Byzantium instead (Zosimus 2.23.1; Sozomen 2.3.2). Julian visited Troy a few decades later in 354 CE, a few years before he became emperor. He mentioned it in a letter some years later, describing how the bishop of the city showed him around the tourist sites, including statues of Achilles and Hector, the Temple of Athena, and the tomb of Achilles (Julian, *Epistles* 19).

The city's decline was partly due to the growth of the nearby town of Alexandria Troas, which had become the main port of the Troad (see Map 2). Troy itself was no longer located on the coast – the silting up of the river basin meant that the shoreline had receded several kilometres to the north. On a practical level, Troy could therefore no longer function as the key commercial centre of the immediate region. With the introduction of Christianity, the city also lost its role as a religious centre, and the Temple of Athena ceased to be the focus of the Troad league. In addition, the Troad as a whole also became less important as a staging point for trade through the Hellespont. This trade now focused instead on Byzantium, which expanded rapidly after Constantine 'refounded' it and made it into his capital in 330 CE.

Therefore, when two large earthquakes occurred in quick succession around 500 CE, there was little reason for rebuilding. After this point, the population seems to have shrunk considerably, withdrawing mostly to the citadel mound once more. The site seems to have been completely abandoned by the start of the seventh century, although there was some limited reoccupation between the ninth and the eleventh centuries. It seems at this time Troy was used as a lookout and a staging post, and would have been a strategic position in the skirmishes back and forth between the Byzantines and the Selcuk Turks.

Over the centuries, the city of Troy gradually faded from memory into myth, and the great metropolis became a quiet agricultural village. The city's complete erasure from the landscape is perhaps best expressed by the words of Byron, quoted at the start of Part Two of this book:

> where I sought for Ilion's walls,
>     The quiet sheep feeds, and the tortoise crawls.

## The remains of Roman Troy

The remains of Troy IX are mostly visible today around the southern edge of the citadel mound. In the Western Sanctuary, at Information Point 10, the new structures of the late first century CE are still visible, including the open-air altar (marked as No. 5 on the information board), and the foundations of the grandstand or viewing podium (marked as No. 11). The new, higher level of the ground in this area is evident if you compare the Roman period altar with the lower altar of the Hellenistic period.

The visitor route through the site passes through the centre of the *agora* at Information Point 11. The *odeion* is still well preserved, and can be viewed here. To the south of the *odeion*, and slightly less well preserved are the remains of the bath complex.

# Part Three

# Icon

What's Hecuba to him, or he to Hecuba,
That he should weep for her?

Shakespeare, Hamlet Act 2 Scene 2, lines 518–19

Shakespeare has his Hamlet ponder the figure of Hecuba, the ill-fated queen of Troy, in one of his most poignant soliloquies. Hamlet wonders at how an actor of his own day can still be moved by the story of Troy, inviting his audience to muse on how and why this ancient tale has continued to resonate through the centuries.

In the final section of this book, we will explore Troy as a cultural icon. After the city fell into ruin in the seventh century CE, Troy came to exist not as a place but as a concept. Over the centuries, Troy has served as a tool for the construction of identity, a symbol of love, a model for war, and a lens through which to reflect on the human condition. Over the next four chapters, we will consider each of these themes in turn.

No attempt has been made, either in individual chapters or in this section of the book as a whole, to be comprehensive. It would be a weighty tome indeed that attempted to chart all the many meanings of Troy through the ages. Instead, I have focused on what I feel are key themes that recur in the receptions of Troy, and particularly important uses of the Troy myth in the period after the city was abandoned. There are, of course, other themes and topics which could have been included, but limited space precludes this. Even within the chosen themes, I have focused on a small number of case studies, preferring to discuss some of their nuances in detail rather than providing exhaustive lists of all relevant examples.

Geographically, most of my examples come from western and southern Europe (to include the countries now occupying the Iliadic lands – Greece and Turkey), although some examples derive from further afield including Scandinavia, the

Americas, and China. This reflects, in general terms, the intensity of interest in Troy as a cultural icon in different parts of the world. It also accounts for the lack of examples in this book from the Arab world. Although there is a rich tradition of medieval Arab scholarship treating Ancient Greek works of natural science and philosophy, Homer and the story of Troy did not occupy a central position within this tradition.[1]

Chapter 11 considers Troy as a source of origins, examining how and why different groups have claimed Trojan ancestry and what this has meant for the construction of national identities. It focuses primarily Europe during the medieval period, from the seventh until the fourteenth centuries, although reference will also be made to later material where relevant.

Chapter 12 is concerned with love, and explores how Troy has been used to reflect on different types of love from romance to desire, from sexual passion to Christian devotion. Its chronological focus is on the medieval period and the Renaissance, from the twelfth to the sixteenth centuries, with some discussion of more modern examples.

The central theme of Chapter 13 is Troy as a setting for explorations of conflict. From conventional pitched battles to culture wars, from sporting rivalries to the verbal debate, Troy has been a byword for conflict in many different forms. The chapter concentrates primarily on the early modern world from the seventeenth to the mid-twentieth centuries, but also considers other cases.

Chapter 14 closes the book, focusing on two themes that characterize much of the response to Troy in the twentieth and twenty-first centuries – tragedy and hope.

Following Hamlet, we might wonder what Hecuba really is to us? Why do we still care about her, her sufferings, and her story? In this final section of the book, we shall start to think about the answers to these questions.

# All Roads Begin at Troy

The tale of Troy was not just a myth about endings – the dramatic end of a city and the fall of a kingdom – it was also a story about beginnings. In particular, it provided a foundation myth for several dynasties, states, and ethnic groups during the medieval period. For several centuries, tracing one's ancestry back to Troy was all the rage.

We have already seen how the Trojan War became a source of origins in the ancient world. In Chapter 8, we discussed how stories of the *nostoi* – the journeys of the Achaean heroes returning from Troy – became foundation myths for many new settlements in the expanding Greek world. In Chapter 9, we saw how the Trojan War became a chronological marker for the start of history. In Chapter 10, we considered how the story also offered an account of Roman origins, with Aeneas and the refugee Trojans settling in Italy and becoming the ancestors of the Romans. In antiquity then, the Trojan War was the 'Big Bang' from which the classical world was thought to have emerged. It provided an explosive scattering impulse which dispersed both Achaeans and Trojans across the Mediterranean, creating the Greco-Roman world as we know it.

The shared heritage of the Trojan War was therefore something that tied Greeks and Romans together, despite the two groups claiming ancestry from opposing sides of the mythical conflict. As we have seen in Chapter 2, the *Iliad* itself acknowledges no substantive cultural differences between the Achaeans and the Trojans, and much of the later Trojan War tradition focused on shared experiences of pain, fate, and suffering. The story of the Trojan War therefore provided a singularly powerful historical connection between the imperial power of Rome and the colonized Greeks that could not be claimed by Rome's other subjects. The story is therefore one of the elements which binds the Greco-Roman world together into a coherent entity, and makes it distinct from the ancient Near East and ancient continental Europe.

After antiquity, the idea of Troy as a source of origins became important again in medieval Europe. The story was widely known, not through the Homeric poems, but rather through a number of later texts which offered summaries or retellings of the Trojan War myth.[2] Over the course of the medieval period, the traditions around these texts expanded ever wider, and were put to increasingly more political uses. Indeed, by the end of the twelfth century, it was possible for the British chronicler Henry of Huntingdon to suggest that most of the peoples of Europe now claimed descent from Troy (Henry of Huntingdon, *History of the English* 7.38). While it might seem somewhat fanciful and perhaps even ridiculous to us, these claims were an important part of the political landscape of medieval Europe.

## Early claims to Trojan origins

Between the seventh and the early twelfth centuries CE, several different claims were made to Trojan ancestry by European noble houses, royal dynasties, and national chroniclers. It should be noted that the existence of these claims in historical writings and literary texts does not automatically mean that they were widely believed by the general population. Other stories of origin were always in circulation, although the idea of Trojan heritage seemed to be particularly popular.

Perhaps the earliest securely known claimant to Trojan origins was the Burgundian chronicler referred to as Fredegar, writing in the 650s. According to Fredegar, the Franks of his own day were descended from the refugees of Troy. While one part of these Trojan exiles became the Macedonians of Alexander the Great, the other was initially known as the Frigii (Phrygians), and wandered widely through Asia before entering Europe. These Frigii elected a king from their own number named Francio, who led them to settle finally in the lands between the Rhine, the Danube, and the sea. It was from this Francio, claimed Fredegar, that the Franks drew their name (Fredregar, *Chronicle* 2.4-5).[3]

A rival tale of Trojan ancestry emerged in the work of the tenth-century German chronicler, Widukind of Corvey. Widukind followed Fredegar in claiming that the Trojans, having been expelled by the Greeks, were the ancestors of the Macedonian soldiers of Alexander the Great. The Saxons, he claimed, were the progeny of the dispersed Macedonian army, and therefore descended from the noblest and most ancient of bloodlines (Widukind, *Deeds of the Saxons* 1.2).

Another German historian, Frutolf of Michelsberg, boasted Trojan origins for a different Germanic group, the Teutons, in the eleventh century. Frutolf's history was expanded in the early twelfth century by Ekkehard of Aura, and is often referred by his name or as Frutolf-Ekkehard. According to this chronicle, the Trojans went first to Pannonia (modern-day Austria and Hungary), where their Roman overlords gave them the name 'Franci'. These Franks eventually fled, fearing a reprisal for the killing of Roman officers, and came to the land of Germany. A subgroup of them went on the run once more soon after, leaving Germany for Gaul (modern France), again fearing Roman aggression. This group, Frutolf argued, were not really Franks at all, but little Franklings (he calls them 'Francigenae'), whereas the true Franks (which he calls 'Franci') remained in Germany and became the Teuton nobility (Frutolf-Ekkehard, *Universal Chronicle*, in Pertz 1844, 115–6).

An entirely different Trojan genealogy appears in the ninth-century writings of Nennius. Nennius claimed that the British were descended from Brutus, the grandson of Aeneas, and technically a Roman (Nennius, *History of the Britons* 2.10). The text offers us two potentially conflicting explanations for how Brutus came to settle in Britain. He is first said to be a Roman general who subdued both Spain and Britain; and he is later said to have been exiled from Italy for accidentally killing his father, arriving in Britain via France where he founded the city of Tours. Around the same time in the ninth century, the Bretons of northern France also traced their origins back to the same Trojan Brutus.[4]

The Welsh cleric Geoffrey of Monmouth elaborated on Nennius' story in his *History of the Kings of Britain*, written in the early twelfth century. Geoffrey claimed that Brutus was the great-grandson of Aeneas, and repeats Nennius' tale of his banishment from Italy after the accidental killing of his parents. But instead of sending him straight to Britain through France, Geoffrey has Brutus travel first to Greece. Here, he is hailed as a leader by the scattered remnants of the Trojans, who task him with leading them to a new homeland where they would be free of the Greeks. Defeating the King of the Greeks, Brutus and the valiant Trojans then set sail across the Mediterranean, eventually landing in southern France. Fighting their way across France, they founded Tours on the way to Britain. Here they found the place where an oracle had decreed they would build their New Troy or Troia Nova, on the banks of the River Thames. The city of Troia Nova eventually became known as London (Geoffrey of Monmouth, *History of the Kings of Britain* 1).

The Normans opted for a more roundabout Trojan genealogy.[5] Dudo of Saint-Quentin, writing in the tenth century, reported that the Normans were descended from Viking settlers who were themselves descended from the Trojan hero Antenor (Dudo, *History of the Normans* 130). A century later, Guillaume de Jumièges retained the idea of the Normans' Trojans origins, but traced it through a different route (de Jumièges, *Deeds of the Norman Dukes* 1.14-6). Guillaume claimed that the Normans were descended from Goths, and used Jordanes' *Getica*, a sixth-century history of the Goths, to argue that the Goths were ultimately descended from Priam's family (Jordanes, *Getica* 9.58). Crucially, these Norman chroniclers traced a line back to Troy that was distinct and wholly separate from that of both their Frankish and British neighbours.

As well as national groups, a number of noble houses also claimed descent from Troy.[6] These included the Merovingians of France, whose eponymous ancestor, Merovach, was said to be the successor of Francio (fifth to eighth centuries CE) and the Carolingians, who ruled much of what is today France, Germany, and northern Italy (seventh to ninth centuries CE). Trojan heritage was something to be aspired to in the early medieval world. This was certainly influenced by Rome's connection with Troy – medieval groups which asserted a Trojan pedigree could position themselves as the heirs to Rome. But a Trojan heritage was to become even more desirable in the second half of twelfth century, when a series of competing and overlapping claims to Trojan blood were made.

## The politics of Trojan ancestry

The late twelfth century saw an increased interest in the idea of Trojan origins, and their strategic political use. The Plantagenet dynasty was particularly quick to see the political potential of a Trojan pedigree. The founder of the dynasty, Henry II of England, had a genealogical foot on either side of the Channel. He owed his claim to the throne of England to his mother; but had inherited territories in France, crucially including the Duchy of Normandy, from his father. It therefore suited Henry to be able to assert a common ancestry for the British and the Normans, and to argue the benefits of reuniting these peoples under a common ruler. During the first decades of Plantagenet rule, a number of genealogies were produced which explicitly argued that the two strands of Trojan blood ran together once more within the royal veins. These politically-motivated genealogies included the *Genealogy of the Kings of the English* of Ailred of Rievaulx, and the royal lineage recounted in the Nun of Barking's translation of the *Life of Edward*.[7]

The Plantagenets also supported the writing of several popular histories and poems written in the vernacular languages, in which the origins of their two subject peoples were always traced back to Troy. These include: a rendering of Geoffrey of Monmouth's work into French by the Norman poet Wace in the *Roman de Brut*, dating to c. 1155; the history of the Dukes of Normandy in his

*Roman de Rou*, written in the early 1170s; Benoît de Sainte-Maure's *Chronicle of the Dukes of Normandy*, written in the mid-1170s; and Layamons' *Brut*, written sometime in the 1190s. Yet more 'national' histories were written in Latin, the language of learning and high culture. These included the aforementioned Henry of Huntingdon's *History of the English*, commissioned during the first years of Henry II's reign in the late 1150s; and, not long after, Alfred of Beverley's *Annals or History of the Deeds of the Kings of Britain*. Indeed, the Plantagenets' politicized interest in history led to something of a renaissance in historical literature in the twelfth century in Britain and northern France.[8] The claim of Trojan ancestry was a standard feature of the time, so much so that in Britain, a historical chronicle was referred to as a 'brut' – a reference to the assumed starting point for all chronicles, Brutus.

The Plantagenets were not the only noble house to seek political mileage in the idea of a Trojan pedigree. Two continental European dynasties produced competing Trojan genealogies in the final years of the twelfth century and the early years of the thirteenth – the Capetians of France and the Hohenstaufens of Germany. While it is not clear how far the chroniclers of these two houses deliberately responded to each other's work, their histories were both written and revised over a period of several years during roughly the same period, and it is tempting to see a head-on engagement in these claims and counterclaims of Trojan-derived identity.

The Hohenstaufens ruled much of Germany and were on occasion the holders of the title of 'Holy Roman Emperor'. During 1180s, when the dynasty's star appeared to be on the rise, and their chronicler, Godfrey of Viterbo, constructed a complex and elevated genealogy for them (Figure 11.1).[9] Godfrey claimed that the refugees from Troy had split into two groups. One of these, led by Aeneas, had colonized central Italy and founded Rome. The other, led by Antenor, had initially settled in Padua in northern Italy, before moving northwards to Germany to become the forefathers of the Teutonic nobility. A splinter group of these went westwards and became the ancestors of the Franks. Godfrey also went on to claim that Charlemagne, the first Holy Roman Emperor and supposedly a direct ancestor of the Hohenstaufens, had Trojan blood on both his mother's and his father's side (Godfrey of Viterbo, *Mirror for Princes* 21–2).

This genealogy had the effect of marginalizing the French, relegating them to an offshoot of the main German stemma. In this, Godfrey drew heavily on Frutolf-Ekkehard's earlier chronicle, but elaborated on it to highlight the cowardice of the 'Franklings' who fled from Germany to France. Godfrey also made a concerted effort to appropriate Charlemagne, who was often thought of as a Frankish king who belonged in the French line. The lineage given him by

Godfrey carefully avoids the Frankish taint, instead stating that Charlemagne united the two strands of Trojan blood by being a Roman on his mother's side and a Teuton on his father's side. This effectively subsumed Charlemagne and the Carolingians into the line of Holy Roman Emperors. The focus on Charlemagne was due to the Hohenstaufen's central claim of Carolingian descent.

Active at around the same time as Godfrey was the French court chronicler, Rigord. Rigord's patron was King Philippe II Augustus of France. Over the course of the twelfth century, the dynastic marriages and conquests gradually united the territories of many Frankish nobles, and Philippe was able to declare the Kingdom of France in 1190, establishing at its head his own Capetian dynasty. During this process, there was much need for a unifying national myth, and the story of Frankish descent from Troy proved invaluable. Rigord, in the first instalment of his *Deeds of Philippe Augustus* offered an account of the Trojan posterity that was markedly favourable to the French (Figure 11.2). In it, he makes full and liberal use of earlier histories and chronicles, combining them in a wholly new way to provide mythical origins for a good many of the nations of Europe.

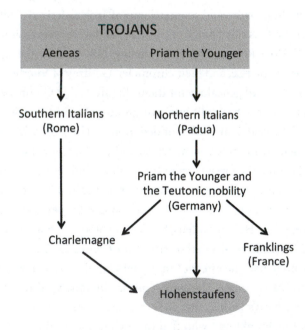

**Figure 11.1** Genealogy of Trojan descendants, as described by Godfrey of Viterbo, *Speculum Regum* 21–2.

Rigord mentions several different groups of Trojans who survived the fall of Troy, descended from five main Trojan heroes – Hector, Antenor, Helenus, Aeneas, and Troilus. The descendants of the minor hero Troilus were said to have wandered east and north to engender the Goths, the Vandals, and the Normans; those of Aeneas settled in Italy. Some of both Helenus and Antenor's descendants were taken as slaves to Greece, but were eventually freed and led to Britain by Brutus, one of Aeneas' grandchildren. Another group of Antenor's progeny travelled with Francio, a son of Hector, to the area of Austria and Germany. After staying here for some time, the descendants of Francio continued westwards to France, while those of Antenor remained in Germany and Austria.

Rigord's version of the Trojan family tree can be seen as a direct repost to the Germanic-centric vision offered by chroniclers such as Godfrey of Viterbo. The Franks of Rigord emerge as occupying the most noble of all the lines of Trojan descent. As a son of Hector, Francio was descended from the most celebrated of all Trojans. The offspring of Turcus were necessarily less glorious, given the minor status of his father Troilus. The descendants of Aeneas, Helenus and Antenor also enjoyed a less distinguished status because these three Trojans were all rumoured to have betrayed their city to the Greeks. The taint of treachery therefore clung to these bloodlines. Out

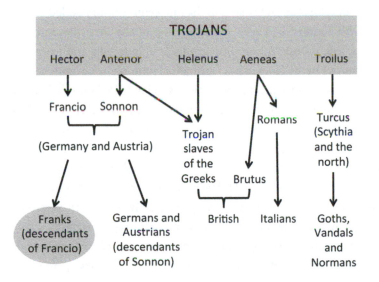

**Figure 11.2** Genealogy of Trojan descendants, as described by Rigord, *Gesta Philippi Augusti* 38–9.

of all the peoples of medieval Europe, it was the French, as the progeny of Francio the son of the irreproachable Hector, who emerged as the 'winners' of this genealogical game.

The overlapping claims made by court historians and royal houses across western Europe in the late twelfth and early thirteenth centuries can be seen as part of wider political manoeuvring. On the international stage, competitive claims of Trojan ancestry were a means of asserting status, and the genealogies proposed for both ruling houses and national populations were a way to symbolically 'get one over' on your neighbours and rivals. Conversely, within composite states such as that of the Plantagenets, the myth of Trojan descent could be used to bring diverse people together. The idea of Trojan origins was used, reused, and misused to such an extent at this time that in the early thirteenth century, all roads effectively began at Troy. This was true even for those who had no political interest in claiming Trojan origins, such as the Icelandic scholar Snorri Sturluson. In his *Prose Edda* of the 1220s, he included a genealogy of the Norse gods which began with Priam at Troy (Snorri Sturlusen, *Prose Edda*, Prologue 3).

## Trojan origins and the Crusades

A further development at the start of the thirteenth century added another twist. The twelfth century had seen the launching of the First, Second, and Third Crusades, where western European armies sought to take and maintain control over territories in the Holy Land. During this time, some Crusaders used Trojan descent as a mean to legitimize their claims to lands in Asia – rather than being foreign conquerors, they were the progeny of Trojans returning to the lands of their forefathers. The narrative really came into its own, however, during the Fourth Crusade of 1202.

Setting out from Venice, the Crusaders laid siege to Constantinople and eventually sacked the city in 1204. The violence of the sack shocked contemporary commentators, with the Crusaders despoiling churches as well as terrorizing the Orthodox Christian population. The reasons for the sack are complex, and include a recent massacre of Roman Catholics in Constantinople by an Orthodox mob, and desire on the part of the Venetians to recoup the money spent on preparing the Crusader fleet. But there was also a deep and long-standing distrust between the Latin Christians of western Europe and the Greek Orthodox Christians of Byzantium. This distrust was now projected back through history to the Trojan

War. The Byzantines were cast as the heirs of the Greeks, who had disposed of the Trojan ancestors of the Latin West through treachery.[10]

Commentators on all sides seemed to cast the sack of Constantinople in this light. This is perhaps most evident in the eyewitness account of Robert de Clari, a French knight who participated in the Fourth Crusade. De Clari reports that a French nobleman was courteously entertained by the Bulgarian king, despite the two fighting on opposite sides of the conflict. When the Bulgarian king expressed puzzlement at the campaign, the French nobleman reportedly replied: 'Troy belonged to our ancestors and those who escaped from it came and settled in the country we come from; and because it belonged to our ancestors, we are come here to conquer land' (Robert de Clari, *The Conquest of Constantinople* 106).[11] Similarly, the German monk Gunther von Pairis described the seizure of treasure from Constantinople as 'the old silver, stained with Trojan blood, [that] conquered Troy, glistening with bounteous wealth, once surrendered to the victorious Argives' (Gunther von Pairis, *History of Constantinople* Lines 12–14, in the poem at the end of Chapter 18).[12]

Writing from the opposite perspective, the Byzantine chronicler Niceatas Choniates used the myth in a pro-Greek manner: 'And these barbarians … descendants of Aeneas, were they trying because of ill-feelings toward you [i.e., the city of Constantinople] to condemn you to the flames that your beauty once lit within Ilion?'[13] The idea of a Trojan heritage justifying aggression against the Byzantine Greeks was therefore familiar, not just to the English and the French, but also for their German allies within the Crusading forces, and to their opponents the Orthodox Bulgarians and Byzantines.

This politics of identity also shaped the way that the stories of Troy were presented and understood, even in contexts far from the political arena. For example, the illustrations accompanying accounts of the Trojan War in medieval manuscripts differed between the Latin West and the Orthodox East. In western and northern Europe, where descent was traced back to Troy, the illustrations often focus on the Trojans. They are usually depicted sympathetically, and scenes of Trojan suffering during the sack of the city are rendered with great pathos. In contrast, manuscript illustrations commissioned in eastern Europe, where affinity was felt with the Greeks, tended to have several important differences. These focus instead more on the abduction of Helen than the carnage at Troy, and tend to exclude scenes of Trojan suffering during the sack of the city.[14] The Troy story was crucial in the shaping of national identities in the medieval period, but national identities were also crucial in the way that the Troy story was understood and interpreted.

## The Trojan Turks

Thus far, I have said nothing in this chapter about one particular group which was often described as being the progeny of Troy – the Turks. A Turkic state, the Sultanate of Rum, occupied most of eastern and central Anatolia by the end of the eleventh century. Turkish occupation in Anatolia gradually spread, with the establishment of smaller principalities or *beyliks* when the Sultanate declined in power. The Troad came under Turkish rule in 1297 with the establishment of the Karasid *beylik*, but was subsumed into the Ottoman realm during its rapid expansion in the early fourteenth century.[15]

The idea of the Turks as the descendants of the Trojans was rooted in the medieval genealogies we have just explored, although it was not until the Renaissance that the theory took more widespread hold.[16] In the seventh century, Fredegar presented the *Torci* or the *Turqui* as an offshoot of the Franks, who split from the main group of Franks during their occupation of Germany-Austria and travelled eastwards to settle in Scythia and the area of the Black Sea (Fredregar, *Chronicle* 4.45–6). The story was taken up once more during the twelfth century, when interest in Trojan origins was intensifying, in the *Chronicle* of Hugh of St Victor. Hugh names Turcus as one of the offspring of Francio, and claims that he gave his name to the tribe who followed him. As we have already seen, Rigord elaborated on the genealogy of Turcus, making him a son of the minor Trojan prince Troilus (Figure 13.2), and placing his descendants in the far north. Rigord's version of the Turkish-Trojan genealogy proved extremely popular in the centuries that followed, and was repeated by the monks of St Denis in their *Grand Chronicles of France* as well as by several other historians.

Therefore, when enquiring into the origins of contemporary Turks, chroniclers and historians proposed that they had returned to Anatolia from Scythia. This was first suggested by the cleric William of Tyre in the twelfth century, who criticized the Turks' abandonment of civilized ways and their descent into barbarity while in the northern Scythian wastes (William of Tyre, *Chronicle* 114–5). This theory was repeated several times in the fourteen and fifteenth centuries, including by the Venetian doge Andrea Dandolo (Dandolo, *Chronicle* 87), and Bishop Antoninus of Florence (Antoninus of Florence, *Chronicle* Vol. 1. Fol. 18r).

Around the same time, the practice of referring to the Turks as *Teucri* – a Latin word that was used of the Trojans – became widespread across western Europe. Political reports and diplomatic correspondence at the time were written in Latin, and these in particular used the terms *Teucri* and *Turci* interchangeably.[17] This state of affairs lasted for several centuries, and after the Ottomans conquered Constantinople in 1453, even more authors were drawn to the Turkish-Trojan equation. At this point, the Turkish sack of the city was seen as revenge for the Greek destruction of Troy. Commentators who followed this line included both critics who bemoaned the sack, such as the Venetian governor of Corfu, Fillipo da Rimini; and 'philoturk' scholars who portrayed the Turkish takeover in an entirely positive light, such as Giovanni Mario Filelfo in his epic poem the *Amyris*.[18]

Attributing a Trojan origin for the Turks was a way of fitting them into a western world view, making them a part of the wider family of European nations. It was an effective strategy for medieval Europeans, seeking to make sense of the growing power of the Ottomans and to fit them into a conceptual world order. As much of Europe was claiming Trojan ancestry, the Turks could be 'made into' Trojans too.

This was politically appropriate at certain points in history, but less so at others, and we find the idea of the Turks' Trojan heritage repeated or refuted at several key points in history. In particular, as the Ottomans began to establish themselves as a European power in the mid-fifteenth century, they began to represent a more imminent threat to western Europe. This triggered some high-profile rejections of the Turks-as-Trojans theory, and attempts to distance the Turks from myths of Troy.[19] But what of the Turks themselves? Did they ever claim a Trojan heritage themselves?

## The Turkish Trojans

While some Europeans sought to make the Turks Trojan in the late medieval period, there is also evidence that some Turks sought to do the opposite – to make the Trojans into Turks. This subtle difference made for an important shift in perspective, one that depended less on the idea of lineage and genealogical descent, and more on the idea of heritage as transmitted through land and culture.

The first possible piece of evidence for this dates to the mid-fifteenth century and takes the form of a letter purporting to be from the Sultan 'Morbisanus'. The letter was addressed to the pope, but it was also published and circulated widely across Europe.[20] In it, the sultan professes affection for the pope and the Italians, who he claims are cousins through the Trojan line. He also states his intention to restore Troy, avenging the sack of the city by subduing the Greeks. There is some debate over the authenticity of this letter, with some scholars arguing that it is entirely fictitious and others suggesting that it was composed on behalf of Sultan Mehmed II, the Ottoman sultan of the time, by an Italian official.

The Ottomans were certainly aware of the myths of Troy. This is most clearly evident from the seventeenth century onwards, when Homer and his account of the fall of Troy began to appear in historical chronicles written by authors such as Ahmed Dede Müneccimbaşı and Katip Çelebi.[21] But this awareness began some time earlier, and can be dated back to at least the fifteenth century and the reign of Mehmed II, the man possibly behind the 'Morbisanus' letter. Mehmed is known to have collected works of Ancient Greek literature, and acquired a spectacular illuminated manuscript of Homer's *Iliad* for his private library. In addition, Mehmed is said to have visited the ruins of Troy.

According to the Greek chronicler of his reign, Michael Critoboulos, the sultan visited the site of Troy when he was pacifying the region around Constantinople (Critoboulos, *History of Mehmed the Conqueror*, in Riggs 1954, 181–2). Marvelling at the ruins, Mehmed apparently claimed that he was the divinely appointed avenger of Troy, and had punished the Greeks for their treatment of the city and 'us Asians'. Although this episode sits well with what we know of Mehmed himself, the anecdote in Critoboulos is nonetheless apocryphal. Indeed, we have no official Ottoman sources which make reference to the episode, and for many centuries there is no further evidence for the Turkish claiming of Troy.

Such a claim did not emerge again until the early twentieth century, in the aftermath of the Ottoman Collapse and the forging of the modern state of Turkey. The Battle of Dulumpınar was one of the final engagements of the Greco-Turkish War of 1919–22, a war known in Greece as the 'Great Catastrophe' and in Turkey as the 'War of Independence'. After his decisive victory in this battle, Mustafa Kemal Atatürk, the charismatic leader who was instrumental in the making of modern Turkey, is reported to have said: 'Now we have taken revenge for Hector'.[22]

In the decades that followed, Atatürk was central in promoting a new historical movement, known as the *Turkish History Thesis*. This thesis had two central tenets. First, it claimed that the Turks had migrated from Central Asia to Anatolia in many successive waves throughout history, and that Anatolia was therefore a Turkish land from its earliest prehistoric occupation. Second, it claimed that Anatolia, rather than Mesopotamia, was the cradle of civilization. In this context, archaeology became crucial in the construction of the new Turkish identity, and the antiquity of Anatolia became a central part of Turkish nationhood. As a result, the Trojans became recast as proto-Turks, creators of an advanced civilization that was brutally but only temporarily destroyed by the marauding Greeks.[23] Homer was also incorporated into this new vision of Turkish prehistory. As an inhabitant of Anatolia, supposedly coming from either Izmir (ancient Smyrna) or Colophon, Homer was considered to be fundamentally Anatolian rather than Greek, and therefore also a proto-Turk.

The *Turkish History Thesis* was gradually abandoned in the 1940s and 1950s, but a strong sense of connection to the ancient past of Anatolia remains in modern Turkey. A beer called 'Troy Pilsner' is brewed and marketed widely. One of the major intercity bus companies takes its name from the Turkish version of the word 'Troy' – Truva Turizm – and uses a depiction of the wooden horse as its logo. And in April 2016, a new electronic payment system was introduced countrywide, under the brand name 'Troy'. The myth and the motif of Troy are still a part of the wider Turkish story.

The special place of the Trojans is such that they can still stimulate controversy. In the wake of the 2004 Hollywood movie, *Troy*, a conversation was sparked in the Turkish media about the relationship between modern Turks and the ancient Trojans. Newspaper columns were written and television debates were staged addressing the issue, and a range of opinions were aired.[24] An argument was sparked between two modern cities, Çorum and Çanakkale, over which held the remains of the Tomb of Achilles. It became evident that, irrespective of any issue of ethnic continuity, the modern Turkish public still feel a close sense of connection with the Troy story. The Anatolian land, rather than genealogy or blood, is the transmitter of heritage and patrimony. The Turks may not necessarily be Trojans, but the Trojans are most definitely Turkish.

# 12

# All You Need Is Love

Love is a central feature of the myth of Troy, and the story of the Trojan War has sometimes been described as the 'greatest love story of all time'.[1] Indeed, on an abstract level, the Judgement of Paris can be seen as a metaphor for the victory of love (as personified by Aphrodite) over the other things that might be desired in life – wisdom (as personified by Athena) and power (as personified by Hera). Small wonder, then, that Troy has often been used as a setting for stories of love.

The English word 'love' has a range of different meanings, however, and there are many different sorts of love that are relevant to the story of Troy. From the passionate love that drove the affair between Paris and Helen, to the protective love of family and home that motivated Hector; from Achilles' self-destructive devotion to Patroclus, to Agamemnon's lust for power; love drives many of the key plot points in the myth of the Trojan War.

The one type of love that is notably absent from the *Iliad* and other early Greek accounts of the tale is the kind of romantic, idealizing love that we usually associate with the word today. Our idea of an all-encompassing love that is not only sexual but also emotional and spiritual is not an original feature of the story. We owe this vision of romantic love, not to Homer, but to the literature of the early medieval period and in particular to the chivalric romances of the twelfth and thirteenth centuries.

## Love and romance

We have already seen in Chapter 11 how the story of Troy was widely known during the medieval period, and enjoyed particular popularity from the twelfth century onwards. This was in part due to Troy's political appeal, and its use in the construction of national and dynastic identities. But it was also due to an explosion of interest in romance literature, much of which used the myths of Troy as a setting for romantic and chivalric storytelling.

Building on earlier traditions of *chansons de geste* (literally, 'songs of great deeds'), the work that really established Troy as a cornerstone of medieval romance was the *Roman de Troie*, composed by the French historian and poet Benoît de Sainte-Maure *c.* 1160 CE. Crucially, it was written, not in the scholarly language of Latin as most works of literature at the time, but in the vernacular French. The *Roman de Troie* quickly became popular across medieval Europe, and translations rapidly appeared in Latin, German, Dutch, Italian, Spanish, and modern Greek. Indeed, the popularity of the poem was such that it spawned an entire new genre of literature focused on the ancient world, addressing in particular what was known as 'the Matter of Troy' (i.e, the subject of the Troy myths). As one modern author has put it, at this time there was 'a pan-European fashion for the wildly popular and ideologically powerful bestsellers with a Trojan theme'.[2]

A central feature of these Trojan bestsellers was chivalric notions of courtly love or romance. Love, as personified particularly by the winged god Amors (a version of the Roman Cupid and the Greek Eros), drives every subplot within the *Roman de Troie*. Four tragic love stories form the focus of the poem – the prehistory of the tale is told through Medea and Jason; the affair between Helen and Paris starts the war itself; Cressida and Troilus play out their romance during the course of the conflict; and the ill-fated love of Achilles for Polyxena, the youngest daughter of Priam and Hecuba, brings about its conclusion. For Benoît, love was both the reason to fight and the reason to abstain, the reason to live and the reason to die.

But Benoît's notion of love was not just a matter of sexual attraction or emotional attachment – it was also the fullest expression of romance or *courtesie*. For Benoît, *courtesie* included not just correct and honourable behaviour in war and love, but also beauty, sophistication, and refinement. And in the *Roman de Troie*, it is of course the Trojans who embody the pinnacle of courtly *courtesie*.

The 'Chambre de Beautés', where the wounded Hector is nursed, is the epitome of these qualities.[3] It is described as being made from alabaster and filled with wonders and luxuries. These included four automata standing in each corner of the room which had mystical powers. The first could show people how they should best be dressed, the second was able to entertain and inform, the third could play music that ennobled the emotions, and the fourth offered counsel on important decisions. The chamber therefore was not only an exemplar of idealized sophistication and refinement, but it was also a means of improving and heightening the *courtesie* of all those who entered into it. The description of the chamber occupies a vital position in the poem as a whole – it is located at the crucial turning point in the story when the Trojans start to weaken in the absence of their hero Hector, and it occupies over 300 lines at the metrical centre of the text (V. 14,631–14,958). It is also mentioned no less than three times in the resumé before the start of the main poem.

The divergence between the image of courtly love at Troy presented in the medieval romances and the earthier erotics of the Ancient Greek sources is notable. As we have already noted in Chapter 11, at this time the Homeric poems were relatively little known, and so Benoît and other western European authors drew much of their knowledge of the Troy story from other later sources.[4] The insertion of romantic love into the myth was an innovation of the medieval period, however, and the reasons behind it are rooted in the changing world of medieval Europe.

The ideal of *courtesie* as showcased in the Trojan romances created a vision of the nobility set apart by their behaviour, manners, and conduct. At a time when new states were being forged and the idea of Trojan ancestry was catching on like political wildfire, the Trojan romances must have had great ideological potential. While these popular works rarely engaged in the particulars of contemporary geopolitics, they did redefine what it meant to be noble – linking it to comportment and conduct as well as to birth and wealth.[5] The significance of Troy specifically in all this must have been linked to the role played by Trojan genealogies in the politics of the time. At the same time as states and rulers were co-opting Troy for their own gain, in the popular culture of the time Troy was made to stand for moral and behavioural ideals.

In the medieval period therefore, Troy was not only a favoured setting for tales of love, but also a world of romance in the wider sense – romance that went beyond love and extended to all areas of life and lifestyle. Troy was therefore the ultimate romantic backdrop – a place where *courtesie* and chivalric ideals reigned supreme.

## Love beyond romance

If Troy in the medieval period was a place where romance went beyond love, it was also a setting where love could be explored beyond romance. Written in the mid-fourteenth century, Geoffrey Chaucer's long poem *Troilus and Criseyde* uses the myth of Troy to set up an ideal of love that goes beyond the amorous passions.

The story of Troilus and Cressida, although not part of the ancient myths surrounding Troy, was well known in medieval Europe as it featured not only in the *Roman de Troie* but also in other works such as Boccaccio's *Il Filostrato*. According to the medieval tradition, the young Trojan lovers are separated when Cressida is sent as a hostage to her father, a defector serving in the Greek camp. Cressida then transfers her affections to the Greek hero Diomedes, forgetting her previous love for Troilus.

Chaucer's particular treatment of the tale is particularly interesting from this point onwards. Upon learning of Cressida's betrayal in the final book of the poem, the hapless Troilus goes uncaring to meet his death at the hands of Achilles. Chaucer does not end the poem with the death of Troilus however – after this event, the poem continues for another sixty-three lines. In the first few stanzas of these, Troilus' ghost reflects on the insignificance of worldly love and the smallness of 'this litel spot of erthe' (Chaucer, *Troilus and Criseyde* 5.1815). The final stanzas return to the narrator's voice, who claims to direct his work at 'yonge fresshe folks' (ibid. line 1835) and encourages them to a new kind of love – the love of the Christian God.

> And loveth him, the which that right for love
> Upon a cros, our soules for to beye,
> First starf, and roos, and sit in hevene above;
> For he nil falsen no wight, dar I seye,
> That wol his herte al hoolly on him leye.
> And syn he best to love is, and most meke,
> What nedeth feyned loved for the seke?

> Chaucer, *Troilus and Criseyde* 5.1842–8

In this stanza, the audience is encouraged to give their love, not to humans who are fallible, but to Jesus: he who (in a loose translation of the Middle English text) 'suffered on the cross for the sake of love, suffered to lift up our souls; who died, and rose, and now sits in heaven above'. The implication is that Jesus has already demonstrated superior love through his suffering, and that love is now due to him in return. Unlike Cressida, Jesus will 'not treat falsely anyone who sets their heart fully on him'. Chaucer completes the stanza by pondering what need there might be for any love other than the love of God: 'and since he is the best and gentlest to love, what need is there for any other false love?'

Troy proves a suitable place to locate Chaucer's story of dysfunctional love. The entire war is a result of falsity in love, reflected in the microcosm of Cressida's infidelity. The pre-Christian setting of antiquity makes this failure of love all but inevitable – if true love is devotion to the divine, perhaps Troilus' romantic hopes were always destined to fail.

## Desire in the eye of the beholder

As well as love in the emotional sense, the myth of Troy has also proved fertile ground for thinking about desire, lust, and sexual politics through the ages. Nowhere is this more evident than in the depictions of Helen, the most famous (anti)heroine of the story.[6] Over the centuries, Helen has been used to explore questions of culpability and blame, causation and inevitability, as well as femininity and feminism. This was true in antiquity, with famous orators such as Gorgias sometimes writing in the voice of Helen as a means of testing their rhetorical skill (Gorgias, *Encomium of Helen*). It was also true in Renaissance Europe, when gender roles were in flux and sexual politics was undergoing a transformation.[7]

Jacopo Tintoretto's painting of 1578–9, *The Rape of Helen*, portrays a Helen carried off by force amidst turmoil and bloodshed (Figure 12.1). Helen herself is being physically dragged by her assailants onto a boat in the bottom left-hand corner of the painting while behind her, scenes of conflict and chaos fade into the background. The composition is marked by diagonal movement and chiaroscuro, with the figure of Helen picked out by the brightness of her head and torso as she reaches for help.

This Helen is not a figure of romantic love or a focus for *courtesie*, nor is she a spur to spiritual devotion. Indeed, in this painting she is not a subject but an object – of Paris' erotic desire, of the physical violence of the soldiers manhandling her, and of the viewer's gaze. It is this final objectification which is perhaps the most illustrative. The brightness that draws the eye to Helen is that of her bare flesh – her naked arms and décolletage almost glow against the darkness of the boat, and the pink hint of a nipple emerges from her dress. The viewer is presented with a tantalizing image – not just of the most beautiful woman in history, but of her becoming undressed. The image teases its audience, enticing the viewer rather than revealing a fully bare breast. Tellingly, Paris is nowhere in view. Rather, his is the voyeuristic gaze that we assume, as Tintoretto tempts us to imagine possessing Helen for ourselves.

**Figure 12.1** The Rape of Helen, by Jacopo Tintoretto, 1578–9.

A comparable image, but one that takes a very different approach to the depiction of desire, was produced some forty years or so later in Ming Dynasty China, in the medium of embroidery (Figure 12.2). This embroidery is one of a set of seven which were made in China during the early seventeenth century using traditional embroidering techniques, but which drew on western imagery to create a hybrid visual style.[8]

Here, Helen appears at the very centre of the scene, surrounded on all sides by a sea of flailing limbs as her assailants bear her away. In this image, Helen's desirability is not signalled by the titillating exposure of flesh, but by her adornments. Helen is literally dripping with gold and precious stones, from her earrings and necklace to her bracelets, from her crown to her girdle. Her dress was also visually arresting – it was originally thinly pinstriped with gold thread, which would have had the effect of glistening and shimmering with an almost tactile quality. Helen would have shone from the centre of the picture, her status as an object of desire draped about her person. What draws the viewer to *this* Helen is not the sexuality of her bare flesh, but the sumptuousness of her accoutrements.

Despite being physically carried away by two soldiers, Helen still dominates this scene. Her gaze, directed upwards to the heavens, is followed by all the figures surrounding her. The two soldiers carrying Helen, the white-haired man behind her thought to be Menelaus, and the wreathed man on the boat thought to be Paris – all have fixed their eyes at the point where Helen is looking. Unusually in visual depictions of Helen, she is in control of the politics of seeing and being seen.

The embroidery dates from a period of gradual decline during the twilight years of Ming Dynasty. The emperor at the time had withdrawn from public life, and Chinese politics were dominated by court intrigues. The arrival of Jesuit missionaries in the sixteenth century had brought not only Christianity, but also new artistic trends and new social ideas. It seems that while incorporating European influences, this embroidery may also be questioning the attraction of western novelties. Helen's desirability in this scene is far removed from the passive sexuality of the Tintoretto painting. It is worldly and materialistic, standing for the desires of acquisition and ambition as much as for sexual passion. Paris thinks that he is carrying off the golden Helen, but perhaps it is he who is getting carried away.

**Figure 12.2** *The Rape of Helen*, Chinese embroidery, early seventeenth century.

## The return to romance

Desires of all kinds seem to have featured in Renaissance portrayals of the Troy story. But the ideal of romantic love was never far away, and romance has once more been at the heart of popular retellings of the Troy myth over the last century.[9]

Two Hollywood movies, *Helen of Troy* (1956) and *Troy* (2004), have focused on romantic storylines – primarily that of Helen and Paris, but also that of Briseis and Achilles. The 2003 UK television drama, *Helen of Troy*, was similarly romantically centred. So too were the 1995 short animation feature, *Achilles*, and the 2012 novel, *The Song of Achilles*, both of which focused on the homosexual relationship between Achilles and Patroclus. Interestingly, modern treatments of the story in languages other than English are sometimes less concerned with romantic themes. For example, the Italian films *La Caduta di Troia* (1911), *La Guerra di Troia* (1961), and *L'Ira di Achille* (1962) include love interests, but the romantic storylines are subordinated to the martial plots.

It is thought that the romance of the myth also lies behind the popularization of 'Troy' as a personal name in mid-twentieth-century America. The name enjoyed a particular spike in popularity in the 1950s and 1960s, following the success of the Hollywood actor and heart-throb, Troy Donahue. Donahue's first name had originally been Merle, but this was rapidly changed by his Hollywood agent, Henry Wilson. Wilson chose the name 'Troy' instead, primarily for its romantic associations. When interviewed on the subject later in life, Donahue remembered: 'at first they had Paris, the lover of Helen of Troy, in mind. But I guess they thought they couldn't name me Paris Donahue because there was already a Paris, France and Paris, Illinois'.[10]

# War: What Is It Good For?

Conflict is central to the myth of Troy and lies at the heart of its poem, the *Iliad*. This conflict of course includes war in the traditional sense – large-scale military confrontations involving the clash of armies and the violent death of many combatants. But as we saw in Chapter 2, the theme of conflict runs even deeper through the Troy myth. The *Iliad* in particular focuses on conflict at several different levels – between societies, within societies, and inside the minds of individuals.

It is perhaps unsurprising that conflict is also at the heart of the way Troy is understood today, and also the way it has been understood through the centuries. At its most basic level, the Trojan War is almost a byword for conflict on a grand and epic scale, and comparisons with Troy are a means of emphasizing the size and significance of a conflict. Likening any recent battle with Troy has the effect of lending it the lustre of legend. When an anonymous thirteenth-century chronicler wrote about the siege of Acre during the Third Crusade, he claimed that it was an epic battle to rival that of Troy (Anon., *Itinerary of the Pilgrimage and Deeds of King Richard*, Prologue and Chapter 32). 'If the ten-year war made Troy famous', he suggests, 'eternal fame will surely extol Acre, for which in like manner the whole world flower together'.[1] Implicit in this comparison is not just a comment on the scale and significance of the conflict, but also a statement about its future fame. Epic scale and significance, it is suggested, would also lead to epic status. Troy, it seems, always meant more than simple fighting.

Indeed, the idea of Troy has been used to explore conflict in many different ways: not just violent combat, but also competition on the sporting field; rivalries in politics; and contests of skill. In almost any situation where one side is ranged against another, seeking to gain advantage, it seems that a Trojan comparison can be applied.

## The conflict within

Troy was used to explore conflict in complex and nuanced ways in William Shakespeare's notoriously difficult play, *Troilus and Cressida*. The play is problematic for a number of reasons. It is uncertain how it should be categorized – it was advertised both as a comedy and a history play when first written, and when the collected plays were published as a folio volume in 1623, it was inserted between the tragedies and the histories without being included in the pagination of either. It is even uncertain whether *Troilus and Cressida* was ever performed publicly in Shakespeare's lifetime.[2]

This may have been largely to do with the play's uncomfortable political message about the failure and fragmentation of state power. In Elizabethan England, the story of Troy was closely connected to the origin myth of the British people (see Chapter 11), and London was styled as a new Troy (Troia Nova or Troynovant). In addition, the Tudor dynasty in particular traced its origins back to Troy.[3] A play set during the Trojan War therefore, and especially one that dramatized the making of controversial decisions, would necessarily have been political. But while the play taps into the general disillusionment that dogged the final years of Queen Elizabeth I's reign, it can also be read as a commentary on the specular fall of the Earl of Essex.

Wildly popular with the general public, Essex had also enjoyed a great deal of royal favour. In late 1597, however, he withdrew from court in a sulk following the appointment of one of his rivals to a position higher than his own. Comparisons with Achilles, already in circulation before this episode, now became widespread. Indeed, when George Chapman published the first translation of the *Iliad* from Greek into English in 1598, he dedicated it to Essex as the 'living instance of the Achileian vertues' [sic].[4] Essex's fall came only a few years later in 1601 when he led a failed coup against Elizabeth's government and was executed for treason. Written in the immediate aftermath of these events in 1602–3, *Troilus and Cressida* uses the ancient myth of Troy to cast a cynical glance over contemporary politics.

Two scenes in particular dramatize dysfunctional decision-making and the diseased body politic.[5] In Act 1, Scene 3, the Greek leaders in council debate the factionalism and disillusionment that besets the army, with Ulysses arguing that what is needed is 'Office and custom, in all line of order' (1.3.88). The Greek leaders then betray the principles they claim to espouse by deceitfully hatching a plot to lure Achilles back to the conflict, by goading his pride and sending

Ajax to his death at the hands of Hector. Later in Act 2, Scene 2, it is the Trojans who engage in a political discussion about whether or not to keep Helen. After making a series of clear and reasoned arguments in favour of returning Helen to the Greeks, Hector eventually reveals that he has already issued a challenge for single combat to the Greeks, assuming a continuation of hostilities.

In both scenes, the characters undermine their own stated positions, their actions undoing the strength of their fine words. The effect is to induce distrust and cynicism in the political process, as expressed neatly by the 'fool' character of the play, Thersites: 'Here is such patchery, such juggling and such knavery! All the argument is a whore and a cuckold' (2.3.68–72).

It is not just the state which is shown to be fragmented and dysfunctional in *Troilus and Cressida*. So too is the self, and the identity of the individual. By the time Shakespeare wrote, the myth of Troy had a rich and varied literary tradition, and he drew on this tradition broadly in constructing his characters. His Achilles owes not only to the wrathful Homeric Achilles that could now be encountered in the English language thanks to Chapman's *Iliad*,[6] but also to the romantic heroes and chivalric models of Chaucer and medieval poetry (for more on which, see Chapter 12). Characters in the play recognize that they are multiple palimpsests of their own literary incarnations. As Cressida tells her lover Troilus: 'I have a kind of self that resides with you, but an unkind self that itself will leave to be another's fool' (3.2.143–5). For Shakespeare, the real conflict of the Trojan War is directed within – amongst allies, between friends, inside the individual.

## The clash of civilizations

At the opposite end of the scale, the Trojan War has also been depicted as a conflict on the grandest scale – as civilizational, rather than civil. As we saw in Chapter 8, in the Classical Greek period it was sometimes depicted as a 'clash of civilizations', a struggle between Europe and Asia, between East and West.

Racial stereotyping, a denigration of the 'East', and the motif of the Trojan War can be found appearing together once more in the mid- to late nineteenth century in western Europe. One example of this is the British politician and four-time prime minister, William Ewart Gladstone. Gladstone was both one of the most influential statesmen of his time and a dedicated classicist with a particular interest in Homer. Whilst serving in government, Gladstone published several books on Homer and the heroic age, and actively supported the excavations of Heinrich Schliemann at Hisarlık.[7]

When comparing Gladstone's Homeric studies with the records of his political speeches and pamphlets, it emerges that there is a striking convergence between Gladstone's views on Troy and the Trojan War on the one hand, and his attitude to contemporary Turks on the other. For Gladstone, Turks were 'one great anti-human specimen of humanity'. He attributed to them four main characteristics. The first was poor government, based on brute force and cruelty. He claims: 'They were represented everywhere government by force, as opposed to government by law.' The second was a superstitious outlook, and the third a lustful sensuality. He stated: 'For the guide of this life they had a relentless fatalism: for its reward hereafter, a sensual paradise.' The fourth characteristic Gladstone attributed to the Turks was a lack of rational intelligence: 'Not even a government of force can be maintained without the aid of an intellectual element, such as he [the Turk] did not possess.'[8]

Gladstone's characterization of the contemporary Turks is remarkably similar to his portrayal of the Homeric Trojans. He claimed that in comparison to the Achaeans, they had a poor form of government, based on kingly force. He stated that his research led him to conclude 'that the same spirit of freedom did not pervade Trojan institutions [as they did the Greek]: that their kings were followed with a more servile reverence by the people; that authority was of more avail, apart from rational persuasion', and that 'the Trojan race had a less developed capacity for political organization'. He also claimed that 'as a nation, the Trojans were much more given to religious observances', and that 'we shall conclude that the Trojans were given to the vices of sensuality'. He also considered the Trojans, like the latter Turks, to be intellectually deficient, as 'in Troy, where there was less of imaginative power'. In general, he concluded, the Greeks were 'more masculine', and the Trojans were a 'feebler' people. On every count, the Trojans were inferior to the Greeks: 'I should say that Homer has, upon the whole, assigned to the Greeks a moral superiority over the Trojans, not less real, though less broad and more chequered, than that which he has given them in the spheres of intellectual and military excellence.'[9]

Indeed, the connection between ancient Trojans and contemporary Turks was made explicit by Gladstone at several points. He explicitly labelled the Trojans as 'Oriental', a term which was more usually reserved for the contemporary Middle East. He also pointed out areas of cultural similarity between Trojans and Turks. In particular, the sexual morality of the two peoples and their inclination for despotic hierarchy, he argued, was similar.[10] Gladstone is only one particularly prominent example of a much wider phenomenon. His conflation of the Trojan past and the Turkish present, and his negative stereotyping of 'Asiatics' in contrast to the 'western' peoples of Europe, is a classic instance of Orientalism.[11] Orientalism, as defined by Edward Said, refers to a mindset rooted in the experience of European imperialism and prevailing notions of race, that created the idea of an exotic but yet dangerous Orient. This mindset, common across western Europe during this period, led to a re-interpretation of the Trojan War as a clash of civilizations – East against West, Asia against Europe – in which the Oriental Trojans were destined, by their very nature, to be defeated.

## Troy and Gallipoli

The story of Troy took on a new significance with the First World War, and in particular because of the Gallipoli Campaign. This campaign was fought between April 1915 and January 1916 and ended in victory for the Ottomans. The loss of life on both sides was considerable however, triggering a broader reflection on mortality and the human cost of war. The geographical proximity of the Gallipoli peninsula to Troy and the Troad meant that many parallels were drawn with the *Iliad* and the Trojan War; before, during, and after the campaign. The lines of mutual influence worked both ways – the Gallipoli campaign became Homeric, while the ancient site of Troy was invested with a contemporary significance.

This is perhaps best known from the poetry written by British and ANZAC (Australian and New Zealand Army Corps) soldiers who took part in the conflict.[12] While references to Homeric epic echo through the poetry of the First World War more general, it was unsurprisingly Gallipoli where the myth of Troy was most commonly invoked. This was done in two markedly different ways. One group of poets used Troy as a means of heroizing the contemporary conflict and representing the entire Gallipoli campaign into a war of epic proportions. On his way to the front lines, for example, the solider-poet Rupert Brooke wrote excitedly in a private notebook about what he felt would be a suitably epic battle. However, Brooke did not live to see the campaign itself, but died of illness while sailing to the Dardanelles.

> And Priam and his fifty sons
> Wake all amazed, and hear the guns,
> And shake for Troy again.

Brooke notebooks; see Vandiver 2010, 242

For several of these poets, the British and Commonwealth troops were cast in the role of the Achaean Greeks, and the Ottoman Turks as Trojans. This identification is in marked contrast to the claims of Trojan heritage made by the British and other European nations during the medieval period (see Chapter 11), and emerges instead from the Orientalist and philhellenic perspectives of the nineteenth century (see above). In these treatments, the campaign itself is seen as glorious and the waging of it as heroic.

At the same time however, other poets were using the myth of the Trojan War in a markedly different way. These poets aim not for glorification, but rather a commemoration of the dead and reflection on mortality. For example, an anonymous poem entitled 'The Dardanelles', published in 1919, collapses the difference between the Achaeans and the Trojans, the Allies and the Turks, and indeed between the heroic dead of epic and the recent dead of Gallipoli.

> How can you grieve? We are not lone,
> There are other graves by the Dardanelles.
> Men whom immortal Homer sang
> Come to our ghostly camp fires' glow,
> Greet us as brothers and tell us 'Lo,
> So to *our* deeds old Troy rang.'

Anon., *The Dardanelles* 11–16

The war dead, past and present, are all portrayed as brothers in death, if not in arms. They are bound together by a common fate and a common humanity. This approach has since come to dominate commemorations of the Gallipoli Campaign.[13] In this context, the Trojan parallel functions as a means of abstracting the dead from their modern political context, and placing them in a heroic commemorative space, beyond the reach of national and ideological distinctions. Indeed, during the grand programme for the fifty-year anniversary commemoration of the campaign, the official state ceremony involved a visit to the site of Troy as a way of reflecting on the broader tragedy of war.[14]

Perhaps the most celebrated example of this approach is the famous poem written by Patrick Shaw Stewart, *Stand in the Trench, Achilles*. Written by Shaw in July 1915 at the height of the Gallipoli Campaign, after three days of recuperation and leave on the island on Imbros, the poem captures the essence of current commemorations of Gallipoli and crucially uses the story of Troy had to lend not heroism, but poignancy. Shaw Stewart was to die only two years after writing this poem, on the Western Front in France. The poem was not discovered until after his death.

I saw a man this morning
Who did not wish to die:
I ask and cannot answer,
If otherwise wish I.


Fair broke the day this morning
Against the Dardanelles;
The breeze blew soft, the morn's cheeks
Were cold as cold sea-shells.


But other shells are waiting
Across the Aegean Sea,
Shrapnel and high explosive,
Shells and hells for me.


O hell of ships and cities,
Hell of men like me,
Fatal second Helen,
Why must I follow thee?


Achilles came to Troyland
And I to Chersonese:
He turned from wrath to battle,
And I from three days' peace.


Was it so hard, Achilles,
So very hard to die?
Thou knewest, and I know not –
So much the happier I.


I will go back this morning
From Imbros over the sea;
Stand in the trench, Achilles,
Flame-capped, and shout for me.

Shaw Stuart, *Stand in the Trench, Achilles*

## Trojan heroism in popular culture

After Gallipoli, Troy had come to stand for the tragedy of war, and in particular for the unity and heroism of the war dead. This is reflected not only in the poetry of the early twentieth century, but also in contemporary popular culture.

Just months after the Gallipoli campaign ended, a new product was launched in the United States which is still responsible for what is probably the most common use of the word 'Trojan' in the United States today – the Trojan brand of condoms.[15] When they were first produced in 1916, Trojan condoms were marketed as a means of protection against disease, rather than as a contraceptive. Packaging was sober and advertising was restrained, focusing on the claim that the brand offered the highest standards and quality.[16] In an era of strict public morality and in the wake of the First World War, this emphasis on martial reliability meant that Trojans were far more successful than their competitors, which tended to market themselves using more romantic or overtly sexual imagery. For pharmacists and consumers alike, Trojans were the honourable (and publicly acceptable) option.

Ideas about honour are also central to the use of the name 'Trojan' for a number of different sports teams in the United States, the best known of which are perhaps the teams associated with the University of Southern California (USC).[17] The name was adopted in 1912 for the USC (men's) American football team, after a sports journalist for the *Los Angeles Times* suggested that it suited the team's heroic efforts.[18] The nickname became popular around the time of the First World War, and the wider university began to embrace the Trojan moniker beyond the sporting arena. In 1930, a statue of 'Tommy Trojan' was set up in the centre of the university campus, referred to in university promotional literature as the 'Trojan Shrine' (Figure 13.1). And in August 2017, a companion statue was unveiled – that of Hecuba.[19]

These two modern uses of the word 'Trojan' tell us something about the significance of Troy in the early twentieth century, especially following the First World War. The imagery used in both cases is generic, evoking the warriors of antiquity in a non-specific way rather than recalling Trojans in particular. But there are many classically inspired names to choose from, so why the name 'Trojan' in particular?[20] What are the particular resonances of Troy and the Trojans?

The answer to this question may lie in USC's explanation for the Hecuba statue. It was Hecuba, they claimed, who urged the Trojans to fight on "even

**Figure 13.1** The 'Tommy Trojan' Shrine, University of Southern California.

when they were outnumbered, exhausted, facing impossible odds".[21] The same ethic emerges from one of the inscriptions on the base of the 'Tommy Trojan' statue – a list of ideal Trojan virtues.[22] This reads: 'Faithful, Scholarly, Skillful, Courageous, and Ambitious'. Unremarkable in itself, the order of this list is significant. It is interesting that a sports team should cite faithfulness as the first and most important virtue, relegating competitive spirit and ambition to the end of the list. What marks the USC Trojans out from other teams then is not their prowess but their sporting ethic – an ethic which stresses faithfulness, reliability, and honour.

Honourable means did not, of course, win out at the siege of legendary Troy. According to the myths, the fall of the city was only made possible by a great and terrible deception – that of the Wooden Horse. This connotation of deceit lies behind the use of the term 'Trojan horse' to refer to a type of computer malware (malicious software). The usage was first coined in 1972 by Daniel J. Edwards, a computer security researcher at the United States' National Security Agency (NSA).[23] The key characteristic of Trojan horses is that they gain access to a computer or a system by deceiving the user as to their true intent. The software usually gets downloaded under the guise of something as innocuous as a receipt, invoice, or other common email attachment. It will then function in an unexpected and malicious way – perhaps corrupting or deleting files, or maybe enabling surveillance or the theft of data. According to Edwards, the idea of Troy just automatically came to mind when he was thinking about this kind of duplicity: '... the useful cover, and then the thing going on underneath, and it was sort of that connection that brought to mind the idea of something which looks good on the outside but has challenges on the inside – Trojan Horse'.[24]

Perhaps the reason we think Trojans are trust*worthy* is because they were famously trust*ing* – in popular imagination they will always be the deceived, and never the deceivers. While Trojans, therefore, are assumed to be reliable and honourable, the idea of Troy in the abstract is necessarily linked with dishonour and treachery. Troy has played a role in shaping, not just in the way we talk about war, the nature and scale of conflict, and the tragedy of war, but also about the way in which conflict is conducted and the competitive ethic.

# 14

# Troy Today

Over the centuries, the story of Troy has meant many things to many people. It has been used to shape national identities and make dynastic claims; to inform moral, romantic, and spiritual ideals; and to further commercial, political, and sporting ambitions. It is beyond the scope of this book to chart all the many ways that Troy has resonated through the ages and to explore all its many meanings. Instead, in this third and last section of the book, I have tried to capture something of the range and flavour of how Troy has served as a cultural icon.

In this chapter, I will focus on how the Troy story has been understood and interpreted in the modern world. Over the course of the twentieth and twenty-first centuries, the world has moved from the confident European imperialism to the horror of two world wars, and thereafter from an era of rival superpowers to one of globalization, decentralization and the erosion of the nation-state. The meaning of Troy has moved with the times, and today, as the twenty-first century comes to maturity, a new vision of Troy is emerging, and the myth of Troy is gaining a new significance.

## Troy as tragedy

As we saw in Chapter 13, after the First World War Troy had come to stand for the tragedy of war and the heroism of the war dead. While more attention is often paid to the latter, it is the former that echoes most strongly in many works of the mid-twentieth century in particular.

This focus on the tragedy of war can be found in Jean Giraudoux's 1935 play, *La guerre de Troie n'aura pas lieu* (The Trojan War Will Not Take Place).[1] Giraudoux sets his play at the start of the Trojan War and depicts a staunchly pacifist Hector in conference with the Greek leaders, desperately trying to prevent war from breaking out. In this play, the conflict is carried out in argument and discussion – the real competition is one of words, and it is in debate that the real victory will be won or lost. As in Shakespeare's *Troilus and Cressida*, in this play deceit and double-dealing also win the day. In the final scene, the treacherous Demokos calls the Trojans to arms, falsely claiming that Ajax has snatched Helen. Hector strikes him down, hoping to prevent the Trojans attacking. But Demokos, in his dying breath, lies once more to place the blame for his own injuries on Ajax. In the final lines of the play, lies defeat the truth and war becomes inevitable.

| | |
|---|---|
| ABNÉOS: | Who has killed Demokos? Who has killed Demokos? |
| DEMOKOS: | Who has killed me? Ajax! Ajax! Kill him! |
| ABNÉOS: | Kill Ajax! |
| HECTOR: | He lies – it was me who struck him. |
| DEMOKOS: | No … It was Ajax … |
| ABNÉOS: | Ajax has killed Demokos … Catch him! Punish him |
| HECTOR: | It was me, Demokos, admit it! Admit it, or I will finish you off! |
| DEMOKOS: | No, my dear Hector, my dear Hector. It was Ajax. Kill Ajax! |
| CASSANDRA: | He has died as he has lived – croaking. |
| ABNÉOS: | There … they have taken Ajax … There. They have killed him! |
| HECTOR | (*removing Andromache's hands from his chest*): The war will take place. |
| | *The gates of war open slowly. They reveal Helen embracing Troilus.* |
| CASSANDRA: | The poet of Troy is dead … the words belong to the poet of Greece. |

Giraudoux, *La guerre de Troie n'aura pas lieu*, Act 2, Scene 14

Once Hector has lost the war of words, the conclusion of the actual war is unavoidable – Hector has lost, just as Troy will be lost. Giraudoux then hits his audience with a final visual message. When the gates of war are symbolically opened, they reveal behind them Helen embracing the young Trojan nobleman Troilus. Earlier in the play, Helen has been depicted pursuing Troilus, in spite of her supposed love for Paris. This act of betrayal on betrayal represents the ultimate fate of Troy, and the total breakdown of the codes of honour and social propriety as embodied by Hector and Andromache.

Giraudoux gives the last words in the play to the prophet Cassandra. She tells us all that we need to know about the outcome of the Trojan War in a typically riddling fashion. She says, not that Troy is dead, but that the *poet* of Troy is dead. It is the poet of Greece, she tells us, who now owns the words. The term in French used here is 'parole', which means more than simply a word. Like the Ancient Greek world *logos*, it also implies an argument, and the act of speaking. In addition, it has the same implication as the English notion of 'keeping your word', in terms of honourable conduct and speaking the truth. In Giraudoux's play, language is both the means of competition and its prize, and the eventual victory of/by/over words is a conquest of truth and morality.

A similar sense of tragedy is evident in the work of the Greek diplomat and poet Giorgos Seferis. In his 1953 poem, *Helen*, Seferis revisits an alternative mythic tradition which claimed that Helen never reached Troy, but was rather held captive in Egypt while a phantom was instead sent to Troy by the gods.[2] Seferis uses this version of the myth to stress the futility of war. His narrator, Teucer, arrives on Cyprus after the fall of Troy, accompanied only by his story.

> I moored alone with this fable,
> if it's true that it is a fable,
> if it's true that mortals will not again take up
> the old deceit of the gods;
>                     if it's true
> that in future years some other Teucer,
> or some Ajax or Priam or Hecuba,
> or someone unknown and nameless who nevertheless saw
> a Scamander overflow with corpses,
> isn't fated to hear
> messengers coming to tell him
> that so much suffering, so much life,
> went into the abyss
> all for an empty tunic, all for a Helen.[3]

Seferis, *Helen* 60–74

Seferis here looks to future wars and future sufferings, with an emphasis on the universality and emptiness of conflict. His sorrowful gaze falls on both Greeks and Trojans, fighters and non-combatants alike, with Teucer and Ajax appearing in the same breath as Priam and Hecuba. Indeed, Seferis offers us Homeric names only to undermine them with the use of indefinite articles. He wonders not about Priam of Troy but 'some other Priam', and not about the Homeric Ajax but 'some other Ajax'. In the future, bodies will fall not into the

Scamander River that flows through the Troad, but 'a Scamander'. This allows us to read into it who and what we will – we could all be Ajax or Hecuba, given the right circumstances. Any pretext could become the cause of war – the Helen or the empty tunic that leads to war. Any city might be Troy. For Seferis, the story of Troy is the story of us all.

Seferis' bleak outlook must have been informed by his own personal experience. Born in Anatolia, he migrated to Greece in the forced population movements that followed the 1919–22 Greco-Turkish War. It can be no accident that Seferis chooses as his narrator in this poem the hybrid hero Teucer, who fought on the Achaean side at Troy, but whose mother was a sister of Priam and who was therefore a first cousin of Hector and Paris. Exiled from his Anatolian homeland, serving his new country Greece as a diplomat, and deeply involved in the politics of Cyprus, Seferis must have seen something of himself in the Homeric Teucer.

The tragedy of Troy is not limited to the war dead, however. In the late twentieth century, the Troy myth has been used by historians and poets seeking for a way to describe other catastrophic events in history. Over the course of the twentieth century, the term '*Troia negra*' or 'Black Troy' has been often applied to Palmares, a community of escaped slaves in Brazil that flourished in the mid-seventeenth century. The early glories of Palmares, and its violent destruction at the end of the seventeenth century, led to it being compared with the mythic city and its history being referred to as 'an Iliad'.[4] In Domício Proença Filho's celebrated Afro-Brazilian poem of 1984, *Dionísio Esfacelado: Quilombo dos Palmares* (literally, 'Dionysius Fragmented: The Settlement of Palmares'), Troy is the metaphorical site for the community, the city that 'agonizes eternal/to the sound/of old carnivals'.[5]

Troy can be used to convey a sense of tragedy even more broadly. *The Fall of Troy* is the title of a song by the American singer-songwriter Tom Waits, dealing with the tragic deaths of the young as a result of urban gang violence in contemporary America. The song, initially released in 1996 on the soundtrack of a film which explores the experience of condemned prisoners on death row, *Dead Man Walking*, uses the tragic resonances of Troy to reflect on untimely death more broadly.

> It's the same with men as with horses and dogs
> Nothing wants to die
> Evelyn James they killed in a game
> With guns too big for their hands

Tom Waits, The Fall of Troy 1–4

# Hope and history

For much of the twentieth century, Troy has been a byword for great tragedy and great suffering. It is perhaps because of this that, in the final years of the twentieth century and in the opening of the twenty-first, Troy has increasingly come to stand for its opposite – the victory of hope over adversity, and faith in an eventual happy ending.

This is perhaps most clearly evident in the afterlife of *The Cure at Troy*, a play in verse by Seamus Heaney, loosely adapted from Sophocles' *Philoctetes* and first published in 1991. The Greek hero Philoctetes, having been abandoned by the other Achaeans on the island of Lemnos because of a festering leg wound, is persuaded in the play to rejoin the campaign against Troy after a prophecy reveals that the war could not be won without him. The 'cure' promised in the title of the play is that of Philoctetes' wound, which stands as a metaphor throughout for human suffering more generally. Philoctetes must first be reconciled, however, with those who abandoned him, coming to terms with the wrongs inflicted on him in the past in order to bring about a cure for his leg and an end to the war.

The play is perhaps best known for a single stanza, which occurs towards the end of the play in a choral ode. The speech reflects first on the wrongs inflicted and suffered by human beings, with explicit reference to both sides of the Northern Ireland conflict through the Republican figure of the 'hunger striker's father' and the Nationalist figure of the 'policeman's widow'. The speech continues on a more positive note:

> History says, don't hope
> On this side of the grave.
> But then, once in a lifetime
> The longed-for tidal wave
> Of justice can rise up,
> And hope and history rhyme.

Seamus Heaney, The Cure at Troy p. 79

For Northern Ireland, as for Philoctetes with his festering wound, a cure is possible – peace is possible. This particular stanza has been frequently quoted, perhaps most famously by the American president Bill Clinton in a speech during the Northern Ireland Peace Process. Clinton was later to use the famous phrase in relation to America as a book title – *Between Hope and History*, published by Random House in 1996 – but during his visit to Ireland in 1995, he deployed it in a number of dynamic speeches which played to the optimism of the time. Heaney had at the time just been awarded a Nobel Prize for Literature, and the peace process seemed like it was about to bear fruit. 'I believe we live in a time of hope and history rhyming', Clinton told the assembled crowds in the city of Derry/Londonderry.[6]

Fourteen years later, in 2009, another American politician was to quote the same poem. On the weekend of his inauguration, the vice president Joe Biden offered quotes from poetry at different events, returning several times to this particular stanza from *The Cure at Troy*. The president inaugurated alongside Biden was Barack Obama, with his buoyant campaign slogan of 'Yes we can!' The zeitgeist was once more one of great optimism. The election of its first black president was seen as a moment of dramatic change and a cause for celebration in a country riven by racial tension. The country, and the world, anticipated the dawn of a new era.

Although in both cases history has not presented us with the complete and immediate transformation that might initially have been hoped for, the widespread popular optimism of both moments in time is striking. Through Heaney, the myth of Troy has become a way of expressing hope and confidence, whatever the history of struggle and suffering behind it.

## The long shadow of a small town

Troy for us today is a symbol both of tragedy and of hope, of terrible war but also of love in all is manifold forms. It stands not only for honour, faithfulness, and heroism, but also for treachery and deceit. It is a fount of origins and identity, a means both of dividing and of uniting diverse peoples.

Troy's status as an enduring cultural icon derives in no small part from this extraordinary versatility. By the same token, much of the flexibility in the Troy story relies on it being instantly recognizable – an allusion or comparison to Troy only works if we know the story of the Trojan War in the first place. Troy's iconic status, then, both depends on and contributes to its position as a common cultural touchstone. This is true today, as it was in the Renaissance when Tintoretto painted his Helen and in the medieval period when Benoît made Troy into a model of chivalry. It was equally true, however, in antiquity itself, when the Roman emperors traced their lineage back to Troy, and the Greek cities configured alliances on the basis of mythic Trojan connections.

Our idea of Troy has changed somewhat since the site of Hisarlık has been identified as the location of the historical city of Troy or Ilium. From the late nineteenth century onwards, we have been confident that Troy was not merely a myth (even if an extraordinarily long-lived and powerful one), but also a real city inhabited by real people. Thanks to over a century of excavation and research, we now know a great deal about these real Trojans, their lives, their stories, and the changing history of their city.

The last few decades have been particularly important for our understanding of Troy as a dynamic and changing community over time. This was not a city that was destroyed and obliterated as is suggested in the myth, but a city of nine lives – a city that went through good times as well as bad, which suffered catastrophe by rebuilding itself many times over a period of nearly four millennia. For most of antiquity, the reality of life within the city of Troy was crucially shaped by the city's myth. From the earliest post-Homeric times, Trojans seem to have been aware of their own heroic past and celebrated it in cult and ritual. The treatment of the city by outsiders was also crucially conditioned by the myth, from the enthusiastic patronage of Alexander the Great and Julius Caesar to the more circumspect treatment of the city by the Persian king Xerxes and the Roman emperor Hadrian.

Recent research has meant that we now know more about this pervasive myth than ever before. We know that there were many wars at Troy in prehistory, and that any or all of these may potentially have formed the basis for the story of the Trojan War. However, we also know that none of these wars matches the legend closely, and that there is certainly more story than history in the tale of Troy. In recent years, we have learnt more about how the tale must have emerged, drawing from rich oral traditions in poetry that recounted tales of great sieges and which circulated widely across Anatolia, the Aegean, and the Near East. We have also come to understand why the story must have come together when it did, in the bubbling cultural crucible that was the eighth-century Greek world.

To uncover the secrets of the myth of Troy, we have had to learn more about Troy as an historical city. In learning more about Troy as an historical city, we have been confronted with the potency of Troy as a cultural icon. And in seeking to understand the nature of Troy as a cultural icon, we must return once more to the myths. Troy, like the greatest of cities, the greatest of stories, and the greatest of symbols, defies categorization. Understanding it is a quest of a lifetime.

# Notes

## Chapter 2

1  Several epic poems in the Epic Cycle do not take the Trojan War as their subject, but were composed around the same time. These are: the *Titanomachy*, which told of how Zeus and the other Olympian gods overthrew the previous generation of gods, the Titans; the *Oedipodea*, which told the story of Oedipus; the *Thebaid*, which told the story of the war between Oedipus' sons and the subsequent campaigns of the 'Seven Against Thebes'; and the *Epigonoi*, which told of the second generation of heroes who fought at Thebes. For the Epic Cycle, see West 2013; and Fantuzzi and Tsagalis 2015. For the Epic Cycle and its relationship to Homeric epic, see Burgess 2001 and 2005.

2  Particularly helpful for reconstructing the Epic Cycle are the *Chrestomathy* of Proclus, the *Bibliotheca* of Pseudo-Apollodorus, and the *Deipnosophistae* of Athenaeus. There are many other later texts which recount stories about the Trojan War, including: the tragedies of Aeschylus, Sophocles, and Euripides; Book 2 of Virgil's *Aeneid*, Books 12–13 of Ovid's *Metamorphoses*; and the *Posthomerica* of Quintus Smyrnaeus.

3  For Homeric poetry and the oral tradition, see Foley 1997; and for orality in Greek culture in general, see Thomas 1992. For oral poetry more generally, see Foley 2002.

4  The relationships between Greek epic and the poetic traditions of the Ancient Near East are not only extensive, but also well documented. For two recent treatments, see Haubold 2013 for the question of Mesopotamian influences on Greek literature and Bachvarova 2015 for a shared oral tradition of epic across Anatolia and the Aegean. The classic work on the subject, however, is West 1997.

5  This fragment has sometimes been used as a basis for arguing the existence of a *Wilusiad* (a Bronze Age epic poem on the subject of the city of Wilusa), which eventually became the *Iliad* (which was an Iron Age epic poem on the subject of the city of Ilion). This is perhaps inferring a little too much from the scanty evidence. See Bachvarova 2015, 21.

6  The role of writing in the composition of Homeric epic has been the subject of much debate. See Thomas 1992, 50–1; Powell 1997.

7  For the ancient debates about Homer, and how this relates to ancient understandings of Homeric epic, see Graziosi 2002; and Graziosi 2016.

8  Debates over the date of Homer are ongoing, see: Grethlein 2010, 122 n3. For the late date of the Epic Cycle, see Burgess 2001, 10–2. For suggested dates for each of the poems in the cycle, see West 2013.

9    For visual representations of the Trojan War story, see Woodford 1993; Lowenstam 2008.

10   This scene appears on a pithos, or large storage vessel, from the island of Mykonos. For the Mykonos Ilioupersis pithos, see Anderson 1997, 182–91. It seems likely that this is an example of a wider tradition in visual representations of the wooden horse – a contemporary fragment of a pithos from the nearby island of Tenos also depicts the legs of a horse mounted on wheels.

11   We may, perhaps, infer something of what such informal traditions may have been like from later sources. For example, the pun on Helen's name in Aeschylus' *Agamemnon* 1476 (*heleptolis* – 'city-destroyer) may have been a common joke. Similarly, Euripides puns on Helen's name to a slightly different effect in the *Trojan Women*: punning with the word *Hellenida*, 'the Greek lands' (lines 876–8); and later with the verb *helein*, 'to capture' (line 1114).

12   For an introduction to the themes of the *Iliad*, see Schein 1996; Lateiner 2004; Edwards 2005.

13   *Iliad* 1.350–427.

14   *Iliad* 9.307-655.

15   Lines 308–430, 607–19, and 644–55, respectively.

16   Descriptions of fighting can be found notably in Books 3–7, 11–17, and 20–1. Achilles' shield is at Book 18.490-540.

17   The poem seems to have acquired this title as early as the fifth century BCE, as Herodotus refers to it as such (Herodotus, *Histories* 2.116).

18   For a discussion of the *Iliadic* portrayal of the city, and of Troy in particular, see Scully 1991.

19   All of these epithets are reserved for Troy alone, and not applied to other cities. See Bowra 1960.

20   Helenus: lines 77–101. Glaucus and Diomedes: lines 119–231.

21   Hecuba: lines 251-96. Paris: lines 325–68. Andromache: lines 398–493.

# Chapter 3

1   As quoted in Heuck Allen 1999, 40.

2   For both quotes and the history of this early exploration of the Troad, see Heuck Allen 1999, 42–7.

3   For Calvert at Troy, see Heuck Allen 1999, 51ff.

4   For biographical details and information about the archaeology of Schliemann, see Traill 1995.

5   For the relationship between Schliemann and Calvert, see Heuck Allen 1999.

6   For Schliemann's own accounts of his work at Troy, see Schliemann 1875, 1881, and 1884.

7    At the time most classical scholars argued that the Greek epic poems, and in
     particular Homer, were not the result of a passive tradition which merely transmitted
     information about historical events through oral history. Instead, they viewed the
     poems as consciously literary creations, composed within an eighth- or seventh-
     century context. The poems would therefore reflect the concerns of archaic Greek
     society, and their contents would owe more to the eighth and seventh centuries
     than to the past events in the heroic period or Late Bronze Age. One notable scholar
     who argued this approach was Ulrich von Wilamowitz-Moellendorff, who set out
     his thinking on Homer with primary reference to the *Odyssey* in Wilamowitz-
     Moellendorff 1884, and later expanded upon this with primary reference to the *Iliad*
     in Wilamowitz-Moellendorff 1916. Needless to say, Wilamowitz was highly critical
     of Schliemann (Calder 1980). This approach to the historicity of Homeric poems is
     similar to that espoused by most classical scholars today.

8    For example, Schliemann is known to have lied in order to obtain American
     citizenship, and to procure his divorce from his first wife. See Traill 1995.

9    For the 'Treasure of Priam', see Traill 1995, 112–26. For Schliemann's own account
     of discovering the treasure, see Schliemann 1874, 289–302 (for the English edition,
     see Schliemann 1875, 323–40).

10   For Dörpfeld's account of his excavations at Troy, see Dörpfeld 1894 and 1902.

11   For the final summaries of the work carried out by Blegen and his team across the
     different levels of Troy, see Blegen et al. 1950, 1951, 1953, and 1958.

12   For Blegen's argument about Homeric Troy, see Blegen 1963.

13   See Korfmann 1997 and Rose 2014 for synthetic overviews.

14   For the lower city, see Jansen and Blindow 2003.

15   Korfmann 2004. In addition, when discussing the visibility of prehistoric ruins
     at the time of Homer in the eighth century, Korfmann also commented: 'I regard
     Homer as a "contemporary witness"' (Korfmann 2000, 23).

16   For Kolb's view, see Kolb 2010. For the arguments of Korfmann and the official
     excavation team, see Latacz 2004. For articles written in direct response to each
     other, see Kolb 2004, paired with Jablonka and Rose 2004; and also Hertel and Kolb
     2003, paired with Easton et al. 2002. For a discussion of the debate, see Cline 2013,
     101–2.

# Chapter 4

1    See Frisch 1975 for the inscriptions.
2    See Bellinger 1961 for the coins.
3    For western Anatolia during the Late Bronze Age and its interactions with the Hittite
     sphere, see Mac Sweeney 2010.

4   It is thought that the Bronze Age form of 'Ilion' was actually 'Wilion'; as Mycenaean Greek included a letter called the 'diagamma' (ϝ), the sound of which approximates to our modern 'w'.

5   See Starke 1997 and Hawkins 1998 for the essential arguments, and Latacz 2004, 78–92 for a summary. Some scholars disagree with the general consensus, see Pantazis 2009.

6   Latacz 2004, 92–100.

7   *Iliad* 2.494–759.

8   For oral tradition as a means of preserving actual history, see Vansina 1985.

9   See the *Annals of Tudhaliya*, in Bryce 2006, 124–7.

10  See the Manapa-Tarhunta Letter (CTH 191 = AhT7), in Beckman et al. 2011, 140–4.

11  See the Alaksandu Treaty, in Beckman 1996, 87, no.13; and Bryce 2005, 226–7.

12  See the Milawata Letter (CTH 182 = AhT5), in Beckman et al. 2011, 123–33 and Bryce 2005, 346–9.

13  The evidence for a king based in the Aegean fighting alongside Wilusa comprises a letter written by a king of Ahhiyawa, which is a term for the states of the Mycenaean Aegean, to the Hittite king. It quotes earlier correspondence and mentions a historic agreement concerning control over the islands of the eastern Aegean. See CTH 183 (=AhT 6) in Beckman et al. 2011, 134–9.

14  The destructions in question end the levels Miletus IV, V and VI. See Greaves 2002, 48–65. The destruction of Miletus V can be attributed to human agency with certainty.

15  For the anti-Hittite coalition, see the *Annals of Mursili* (CTH 61). For Piyamaradu, see the Tawagalawa Letter (CTH 181 = AhT4), in Beckman et al. 2011, 101–22. For the Hittite conquest, see the Milawata Letter (CTH 182 = AhT5), in Beckman et al 2011, 123–33 and Bryce 2005, 346–9.

16  Morris 1989.

17  For the *Song of Release* and its relationship to the *Iliad*, see Bachvarova 2015.

18  Sherratt 1990.

19  See Malkin 2011 for the eighth century as a crucial period for the emergence of Greek identity, in particular with relation to the widening of external contacts and the spread of Greek settlement (sometimes known as 'Greek colonization', although this is a highly problematic term). Hall 2002 argues against the increased contacts of the eighth century as being central to the development of Greekness and, instead, places the emergence of a conscious Greek identity much later in the fifth century, as a result of the Persian Wars. We will address the issue of Greek identity and the Persian Wars in Chapter 8, but for the purposes of this chapter it is enough to note that for the stated reasons, the eighth century must have been a crucial period for the emergence of the idea of Greekness. It was an idea that changed and developed dramatically over time, and which only crystallized into the kind of ethnic identity we recognize today much later, but the roots of the concept can clearly be found in the eighth century.

20   For the emergence of the *polis* and other eighth-century developments in the
     Aegean, see Osborne 2009, 66–130.

# Chapter 5

1    For general overviews of Early Bronze Age Anatolia, see Sagona and Zimansky
     2009, 144–224; and Düring 2011, 257–99.
2    For Troy I, see Blegen et al. 1950, 33–199; Séfériadès 1985; Sazci 2005; and Jablonka
     2011, 719.
3    For EB I as a 'proto-urban' period, see Düring 2011, 263–9.
4    Düring 2011, 266–8.
5    Kouka 2013, 570.
6    Sazcı 2005; Jablonka 2010, 851–82.
7    For Troy II, see Blegen et al. 1950, 203–378; Düring 2011, 284–6; Jablonka 2011,
     719–20.
8    Düring 2011, 275; Muhly 2011, 866.
9    Çalış-Sazci 2006.
10   Şahoğlu 2005, 354; Düring 2011, 272–3.
11   For the 'International Spirit' in the Aegean, see Broodbank 2000, 279–83.
12   At Limantepe for example, one of the better-preserved towers in the fortification
     wall still stands to a height of 6 m: Kouka 2013, 570; Erkanal 1999.
13   Steadman 2011, 240–1.
14   Düring 2011, 283.
15   Steadman 2011, 241; Blegen et al. 1951, 1–97.
16   For the 'Anatolian Troy culture', see Sazci 2005, Blum 2006, and Jablonka 2010, 853.
     For Troy IV, see Blegen et al. 1951, 99–218.
17   Efe 2007.
18   See Steadman 2011, 245–7 for the Anatolian plateau at this time.
19   For what are known as the Alacahöyük 'Royal Tombs', see Bachhuber 2011 and
     Düring 2011, 290–4.
20   For Troy V, see Blegen et al. 1951, 219–98. For an overview of Middle Bronze Age
     Anatolia, see Sagona and Zimansky 2009, 225–52.
21   Michel 2001; Veenhof 2013.
22   For Kültepe, see Özguç 2003. For the merchants' archives, see Veenhof 2000, 83–8;
     Aubet 2013, 307–64.
23   Veenhof 2000, 103–5; Aubet 2013, 267–306.
24   For the 'Burnt Palace' in Level V Beycesultan, see Lloyd and Mellaart 1965. For
     Konya Karahöyük, see Sagona and Zimansky 2009, 247. For this period in Anatolia
     more generally, see Barjamovic 2011.

25  For the fortification wall in this area, see Korfmann 2001, 7–9.

26  Riorden 2014, 440–1.

27  Sazci 2001.

# Chapter 6

1   For Troy VI, see Jablonka 2011, 721–3; Rose 2014, 19–25.

2   For the Pillar Hall, see Blegen et al. 1953, 210–29. For the megaron by the West Gate, see Rose 2014, 24 and Becks et al. 2006. The cultic nature of this building in the LBA is especially significant, given that the same building was later reused in the cultic setting in the Iron Age (see below). The remains suggesting a cult use include: a bronze figurine, a seal from the Mycenaean Aegean, some small pieces of gold, an ivory spindle, and a type of vessel known as a 'rhyton' associated with the pouring of libations, and miniature objects that would have been dedicated as votives. Another building used for cult purposes seems to have been the Anta House, see Blegen et al. 1953, 138–9.

3   It has been argued that the myth of the wooden horse is a metaphor for the earthquake that ended Troy VI, on the basis that earthquakes were presided over the by god Poseidon, who also was the patron of horses. This would allow Troy VI to be Homeric Troy.

4   For the Mycenaean Linear B archives, see Palaima 2010.

5   For the Hittite archives, see Beckman 2011.

6   For archives and texts at Ugarit, see Van de Mieroop 2007, 163–70.

7   The Milawata Letter (CTH 182 = AhT5), in Beckman et al. 2011, 123–33 and Bryce 2006, 346–9.

8   Bachvarova 2015, 21.

9   See the *Annals of Tudhaliya*, in Bryce 2005, 124–7.

10  As claimed by the Alaksandu Treaty, for which see Beckman 1996, 87, no.13; and Bryce 2005, 226–7.

11  For the debate around the kingdom of Ahhiyawa, see Beckman et al. 2011.

12  For trade and exchange in the Late Bronze Age, see Gale 1991; Sherratt and Sherratt 1993; Manning and Hulin 2005; Laffineur and Greco 2005; and Maran and Stockhammer 2012.

13  For the debate over the place of Troy in the long-distance trade of the Late Bronze Age, see Kolb 2004, and Hertel and Kolb 2003 for the argument on Troy not playing an important role; and Jablonka and Rose 2004, 624–6 and Easton et al. 2002 for the rejoinder.

14  For the Amarna archive, see Moran 2000. For the wider international system of the Late Bronze Age, see Van de Mieroop 2007, 130–48.

15  For the Ulu Burun shipwreck, see Bass 1987 and Pulak 1998.

16  Feldman 2006.

17  For these Grey Wares, see Bayne 2000 and Pavúk 2010.

18  For textile manufacture, see Pavúk 2012. For the production of murex dye, see Çakırlar and Becks 2009.

19  See Rose 2014, 36.

20  For Troy VIIa, see Rose 2014, 30 and 36–8; Blegen 1963.

21  The Tawagalawa Letter (CTH 181 = AhT4), in Beckman et al. 2011, 101–22.

22  For the Alaksandu Treaty, see Beckman 1996, 87, no.13; and Bryce 2005, 226–7.

23  See note 21 above.

24  For the dramatic events at the end of the Late Bronze Age, see Bachhuber and Roberts 2012; Cline 2014; Dickinson 2006.

# Chapter 7

1  See the references in Chapter 6, note 24.

2  Astour 1965, 255.

3  For the collapse of the Hittite Empire, see Bryce 2006, 327–56.

4  Langgut et al. 2013.

5  See Hitchcock and Maeir 2014; and Cline 2014.

6  Rose 2014, 34–5.

7  For Troy VIIb$_1$ see Aslan and Hnila 2015, 188–94, and Rose 2014, 38–40.

8  For the Phrygians, see Sagona and Zimansky 2009, 352–62.

9  Rose 2014, 46–50; Aslan and Hnila 2015, 194–205.

10  Rose 2014, 69–71.

# Chapter 8

1  For this phase, see Rose 2014, 50–3.

2  For cult activity in the Western Sanctuary area, see Aslan 2011, 412–6 and Rose 2014, 50.

3  See Aslan 2011 for a comprehensive discussion of the 'Place of Burning'.

4  For the cult activity in D9, see Aslan 2011, 416–20.

5  For hero cult in general, see Antonaccio 1995. For hero cult in Troy and the Troad specifically, see Aslan 2011, 420–5.

6  See Malkin 1998.

7  For this phase, see Rose 2014, 53–69.

8  Alsan 2002; Blegen et al. 1958, 256.

9    Jeffrey 1961 (2003); Blegen et al. 1958, 266, 278, 280.

10   See Rose 2014, 72–142.

11   Anderson 1997.

12   For a discussion of this poem, see Goldhill 1991, 116–9.

13   Translation from West 1993, 96.

14   For Archaic Greek culture, see Osborne 2009.

15   For Troy during this phase, see Rose 2014, 143–57.

16   For Trojans and Persians in the visual culture of Classical Athens, see Castriota 2005.

17   The classic work on inventing the barbarian is Hall 1989. See also Cartledge 1997; Isaac 2006; Mitchell 2007; and Kim 2009. For Greek ethnography before the Persian Wars, see Skinner 2012.

18   For Herodotus and his ethnographic imagination, see Skinner 2012, Thomas 2002.

# Chapter 9

1    For an introductory history of the Hellenistic world, see Shipley 1999 and Erskine 2003.

2    For *koine* Greek, see Colvin 2010, 63–5.

3    For the Battle of the Granicus, the main ancient sources are: Arrian 1.13–6; Plutarch, *Alexander* 16; Diodorus Siculus 17.18–9. For modern scholarship on the battle, see Hammond 1980.

4    For Alexander's activities at Troy, see Cartledge 2004, 137; and Cohen 1995.

5    For the activities of Antigonus and Lysimachus at Troy and developments in the city during this period, see Rose 2014, 158–70.

6    For Troy under the Seleucids, see Rose 2014, 170–95.

7    For the Western Sanctuary area during the Hellenistic period, see Rose 2014, 196–216.

8    For the cult of Cybele, see Roller 1999.

9    For the tumuli of the Troad, see Rose and Körpe 2016.

10   See Rose 2014, 59–60 and 189–90; and Hornblower 2015, 405–12 for a discussion of the Locrian Maidens.

11   For the metopes, see Webb 1996, 47–52.

12   For the Panathenaea at Troy, see Rose 2014, 160–2.

13   Even local potentates and more modest rulers sought to gain cultural capital by establishing libraries, see Johnstone 2014.

14   For Hellenistic literature, see Clauss and Cuypers 2010.

15   For the Laocoön, see Brilliant 2000.

16   Scheer 2003. For *ktsis* poetry, see Dougherty 1994 and Krevans 2000.

17   For the Fimbrian sack, see Rose 2014, 219–21.

# Chapter 10

1 For the Roman Republic, see Flower 2014.

2 For the poverty of Troy during this century, see Rose 2014, 221.

3 Lucan is, of course, indulging in some poetic license here, and is also more intent on describing the poor state of the remains of *ancient* Troy (i.e., Homeric Troy), rather than the contemporary city: see Rossi 2001.

4 For Roman Troy, see Rose 2014, 223–63.

5 For the Julio-Claudian benefactions, see Rose 2014, 223–34.

6 For a discussion of Roman foundation myths, see Cornell 1975; Wiseman 1995; and Squire 2015, 159–65.

7 For the popularity of this image, see Fuchs 1973.

8 This governor was Herodes Atticus, the father of the well-known sophist Herodes Atticus. The family was known for being fabulously wealthy, and both father and son are known for their generous benefactions at Athens. For Herodes Atticus and Troy, see Philostratus, *The Lives of the Sophists* 2.1.

9 See Rose 2014, 247–8 for Hadrian and the Tomb of Ajax.

10 For Hadrian, see Birley 1997.

11 It seems likely that the statue set up by Caracalla is the same as that seen 140 years later by the emperor Julian (Julian, *Epistles* 19). See Rose 2014, 260 for a discussion.

12 For Troy in later antiquity, see Rose 2014, 263–71.

# Part 3

1 Graziosi 2015.

# Chapter 11

2 The Homeric epics were not translated from original Greek until the Renaissance, and therefore enjoyed only limited circulation during the medieval period. Instead, most knowledge about the story of Troy was derived from two late antique novels, both of which ostensibly purported to be eyewitness accounts of the Trojan War: Dictys' *Chronicle of the Trojan War* and Dares' *History of the Fall of Troy*. For the transmission of the Trojan War myths from antiquity through the medieval period, see Aerts 2012 and Desmond 2016.

3 Although it has been argued that this story was also known by Gregory of Tours a century earlier, see Barlow 1995.

4 Bouet 1995, 406.

5 Bouet 1995 and Albu 2001.

6 Beaune 1991, 226. From the fourteenth century onwards, the idea of Trojan origins was exploited to the full by the Hapsburg dynasty, in particular by Charles IV: see Tanner 1993.

7 Aurell 2007, 382.

8 Damian-Grint 1999; see also Albu 2001.

9 Tanner 1993, 88–91; Hering 2015.

10 Beaune 1991, 237; Shawcross 2003.

11 Translation and quotation from Boeck 2015, 267.

12 Translation from Andrea 1997. For a discussion, see Shawcross 2003, 132.

13 Translation and quotation from Beaune 1991, 237–8.

14 Boeck 2015, 266. For the western tradition of illustrating the Troy story, see Buchthal 1971 and Stones 2005. For a summary of where the Troy story appears in Byzantine literature, see Aerts 2012.

15 For early Turkish history, the Sultanate of Rum, and the expansion of the Ottoman Empire, see Fleet 2009.

16 For the Turks in Trojan genealogies, see Meserve 2008, 47–63.

17 Meserve 2008, 26–34.

18 Harper 2005, 157; Meserve 2008, 37–42.

19 Harper 2005.

20 Meserve 2008, 35–7.

21 Uslu 2012, 143.

22 Aslan and Atabey 2012.

23 For the Turkish History Thesis, see Atakuman 2008.

24 See Gür 2010 for a critical discussion and Şahin 2004 for the publication of some of the articles and comment pieces written at the time.

# Chapter 12

1 Winkler 2007, 251 (Plate 15).

2 Boeck 2015, 264. For the spread of the *Roman de Troie* and its popularity, see Young 1948, 63ff.

3 For the chamber, see Sullivan 1985 and Rabeyroux 1992.

4 Notably, the texts attributed to Dares and Dictys, see Chapter 11, note 1. For summaries of the transmission of the Troy myth through the medieval period, see Aerts 2012 and Desmond 2016.

5 For example, the *Roman de Troie* makes no explicit mention of the French as descendants of the Trojans. However, the Trojans are portrayed in a positive light

and with some sense of a proto-national consciousness, see Eley 1991. Bruckner 2015 argues that the poem was also specifically aimed at a Plantagenet audience.

6 For nuanced discussions of the figure of Helen through history, see Maguire 2009 and Gumpert 2001.

7 Weaver 2007.

8 For this embroidery in general, see Denney 2012.

9 For cinematic retellings of the Troy story, see Paul 2013, 37–92.

10 Stark 1984. For the phenomenon more generally, see Solomon 2015, 244–5.

# Chapter 13

1 Translation from Pryor 2015, 97.

2 For the generic complexity of *Troilus and Cressida*, its manuscript history, and a general introduction to the play more generally, see Bevington 1998. When quoted, the version of the text used is that of the Arden Shakespeare, edited by Bevington (1998).

3 See Shepard and Powell 2004. The poet Edmund Spenser, for example, offers a new version of the Paris-Helen romance in the Troynovant of London in Book 3 of his *The Faerie Queene*. See Bates 2010.

4 Chapman dedicated the first instalment of his translation to Essex when it was published in 1598, entitled the *Seaven Bookes of the Iliades*. For Chapman and Essex, see Briggs 1981. For Chapman and his celebrated translation of the *Iliad* more generally, see Sowerby 1992 and Nicoll 1998.

5 On the political cynicism of *Troilus and Cressida*, see Greenfield 2000.

6 There is considerable discussion about the extent to which Shakespeare was familiar with Homer. See Nuttall 2004, Burrow 2013, and Schein forthcoming.

7 Gladstone was one of Schliemann's strongest supporters, and ensured that he received a warm welcome in Britain. For the Gladstone-Schliemann relationship, see Vaio 1992.

8 All quotes in this paragraph are taken from Gladstone 1858; the first three are from p. 3 and the last from p. 10.

9 Gladstone's treatment of the Trojans can be found in the third volume of *Studies on Homer and the Heroic Age* (Gladstone 1958), 145–248. The quotes in this paragraph are taken from the following pages, respectively: 206, 217, 189, 207, 153, and 192–3.

10 See Gladstone 1958. The comparison of a more masculine and a feebler people is on p. 207. The labelling of Trojans as 'Orientals' can be found on pp. 165 and 210, and the comparison with the morality and sense of hierarchy in contemporary Turkey is on p. 211.

11 For the phenomenon of Orientalism, see Said 1978. For the debate around the term, 'Orientalism', see Said's preface to the 1993 printing of the book, and the Afterword of the 1995 edition.

12 For the British soldiers, see Vandiver 2010. For the use of Homer and Virgil by ANZAC soldiers, see Midford 2013 and 2010.

13 As quoted in Rose 2014, 286.

14 Indeed, this reflection on common humanity lies behind a famous letter written by Kemal Atatürk, who led the Turkish forces at Gallipoli, to the parents of the British and Commonwealth dead after the war: 'There is no difference between the Johnnies and the Mehmets to us where they lie side by side here in this country of ours', see Atabey et al. 2016, 227.

15 In 2007, Trojans accounted for 70.5 per cent of all condom sales in American pharmacists, having more than four times the market share of their closest rival, Durex. See Koerner 2006 and Tone 2002.

16 When a rival manufacturer began to copy the Trojan name and packaging in 1926, the original makers launched a number of lawsuits to protect their brand and published a series of advertisements which denigrated the condom 'pirates' and the inferior products they were pedalling. See Treichler 2014.

17 Sports teams elsewhere in the world have also used the name 'Trojan', including: Belfast, UK (American football); Liverpool, UK (baseball); Southampton, UK (hockey).

18 Florence 2004, 201.

19 This statue caused some controversy when it was first unveiled, although not directly related to its Trojan theme. One of the inscriptions on the base is the quote from Hamlet that began this section of the book, with the attribution to 'Shakespear' (i.e. spelled without an 'e'). A public debate was held over the correct spelling of the playwright's name.

20 Other classically named condoms include the 'Atlas' brand, launched in 1997; and other classically named sports teams include Spartans, Gladiators, Caesars, Romans, and Titans. Titans: Tennessee, USA (American football); Centurion, South Africa (cricket); Rotherham, UK (rugby). Spartans: Bridgetown, Barbados (cricket); Michigan State University, USA (all sports); Edinburgh, UK (football); Essex, UK (American football). Romans: Chester, UK (American football); Xanten, Germany (basketball). Gladiators: Quetta, Pakistan (cricket); Trier, Germany (basketball); Atlanta, USA (ice hockey); Cleveland, USA (American football). Caesars: Nottingham, UK (American football); Detroit, USA (baseball). This list is far from exhaustive, and perhaps not even representative, but demonstrates that modern sports teams have chosen a range of classically inspired names.

21 USC President C.L. Max Nikias, '*The LA Times*, August 17th, 2017'.

22 The other inscriptions are: a quote from Virgil in both Latin and English ('Sedes ubi fata quietas/ostendunt: illic fas regna resurgere Troiae: Here are provided seats of meditative joy/Where shall arise again the destined reign of Troy': Aenied 1.205–6); and the university motto ('Palmam qui meruit ferat': let him who deserves it take the palm).

23 Summers 1999, 99; Yost 2013.

24 Yost 2013, 26.

# Chapter 14

1 The play was translated into English as *The Tiger at the Gates* by Christopher Fry in 1955.

2 This alternative myth drives the plot of Euripides' *Helen*, and is also recorded in Herodotus' *Histories* 2.112–120.

3 Translated by Edmund Keeley. See Seferis 1995, 177.

4 For example, Macedo 1963; Landmann 1998.

5 Translation from Kouklanakis 2016, 20. This poem makes complex use of the classical allusions and references far beyond the myth of Troy, as indicated by its title. See Kouklanakis 2016 for a discussion.

6 Archive, United States Government Publishing Office: Administration of William J. Clinton 1995, November 30, p. 1809 (https://www.gpo.gov/fdsys/pkg/PPP-1995-book2/pdf/PPP-1995-book2-doc-pg1809.pdf) retrieved 26 September 2016.

# Guide to Further Reading

The literature available on Troy, Homer, and the myth of the Trojan War could fill an entire library by itself. The following notes are designed to help guide you through this maze of reading, to enable you to explore further the different aspects of the topic that interest you particularly. I have organized this guide into three parts, corresponding to the three sections of this book.

## Myth

So many excellent books have been written about Homer and the *Iliad* that it can be difficult to choose between them. As a starting point, I would recommend Barbara Graziosi's *Homer* (Oxford University Press, 2016), which provides a wide-ranging and up-to-date introduction to the key issues surrounding Homeric epic.

For those keen to delve into the *Iliad* for themselves, the poem has been translated many times into English. The classic translation today is still perhaps that of Richard Lattimore, first published in 1951 and recently reissued with a revised introduction and notes by Richard Martin (University of Chicago Press, 2011). Lattimore's elegant verse captures much of the flavour of the original Greek, although Anthony Verity's more recent translation is closer to the Greek text (Oxford University Press, 2011).

To learn more about the colourful figure of Schliemann, I would turn to David Traill's excellent *Schliemann of Troy: Treasure and Deceit* (St Martin's Pres, 1995). A more general sketch of the excavation history of the site can be gained from Jill Rubalcaba and Eric Cline's *Digging for Troy: From Homer to Hisarlik* (Charlesbridge Publishing, 2011).

Eric Cline's *The Trojan War: A Very Short Introduction* (Oxford University Press, 2013) is a handy guide to the key issues surrounding the Trojan War myth. It is more up to date and therefore preferable to the beautifully written *In Search of the Trojan War* by Michael Wood, which, despite a 2005 reissue, has not been thoroughly updated to take into account recent discoveries (BBC Books, 1985).

## Site

Guidebooks to the site of Troy are widely available, but good summaries of the current state of knowledge can be found first and foremost in Brian Rose's *The Archaeology of Greek and Roman Troy* (Cambridge University Press, 2014). Although, as the title implies, the book focuses primarily on the post–Bronze Age periods of the site, it also offers a comprehensive and nuanced discussion of the prehistoric levels in its first chapter.

Shorter summaries of the Bronze Age remains at Troy can be found in articles by Peter Jablonka: 'Troy' in *The Oxford Handbook to the Bronze Age Aegean* (edited by Eric Cline, Oxford University Press, 2010); and 'Troy in Regional and International Context' in *The Oxford Handbook of Ancient Anatolia* (edited by Sharon Steadman and Gregory McMahon, Oxford University Press, 2011).

There have been many detailed studies of the significance of the Trojan War myth at different points during antiquity, but few overarching or comprehensive works on the subject. Perhaps the closest thing to it is Andrew Erskine's *Troy between Greece and Rome: Local Tradition and Imperial Power* (Oxford University Press, 2003). For individual cases and examples of the Trojan War myth in specific periods and contexts, see the notes in Chapters 8, 9, and 10.

## Icon

The literature on the later receptions of Troy is rich and diverse. Several books offer catalogues of works on a Trojan theme. These include Arthur Young's *Troy and Her Legend* (University of Pittsburgh Press, 1948), which categorizes work by artistic medium (literature, painting, sculpture, etc.), and Margaret Scherer's *The Legends of Troy in Art and Literature* (Phaidon, 1963), which categorizes work by mythic episodes. The latter is especially useful for its long appendix, which lists a great number of works that take a Trojan theme. Less comprehensive is Diane Thompson's *The Trojan War: Literature and Legends from the Bronze Age to the Present* (McFarland and Co., 2004), a very basic guide to key works which may perhaps be appropriate for schools or a younger audience.

Other books adopt a more reflective and discursive approach to the subject. These include Chapter 5 of Carol Thomas and Craig Conant's *The Trojan War* (University of Oklahoma Press, 2005), the essays in *Homer and the Twentieth Century* (edited by Barbara Graziosi and Emily Greenwood, Oxford University

Press, 2007), and the later chapters of *Troy: City, Homer and Turkey* (edited by Jorrit Kelder, Günay Uslu, and Ömer Faruk Şerifoğlu, W Books, 2013).

To return finally to Homer, two recent books offer whistle-stop explorations of the enduring appeal of Homeric epic from a more personal perspective: Alberto Manguel's *Homer's 'The Iliad' and 'The Odyssey': A Biography* (Atlantic Books, 2008) and Adam Nicholson's *The Mighty Dead: Why Homer Matters* (William Collins, 2015).

# References

Aerts, W. 2012. 'Troy in Byzantium', in J. Kelder, G. Uslu and Ö.F. Şerifoğlu (eds.) *Troy. City, Homer, Turkey*, 98–103. Istanbul: W Books.

Albu, E. 2001. *The Norman in Their Histories: Propaganda, Myth and Subversion.* Woodbridge, Suffolk: Boudell Press.

Anderson, M.J. 1997. *The Fall of Troy in Early Greek Poetry and Art.* Oxford: Clarendon Press.

Andrea, A.J. (ed.) 1997. *The 'Hystoria Constantinopolitana' of Gunther of Pairis.* Philadelphia: University of Pennsylvania Press.

Antonaccio, C.M. 1995. *An Archaeology of Ancestors. Tomb Cult and Hero Cult in Early Greece.* Lanham, MD: Rowman and Littlefield.

Aslan, C.C. 2002. 'Ilion before Alexander: Protogeometric, Geometric, and Archaic Pottery from D9', *Studia Troica* 12: 81–129.

Aslan, C.C. 2011. 'A Place of Burning: Hero or Ancestor Cult at Troy', *Hesperia* 80: 381–429.

Aslan, C.C. and P. Hnila. 2015. 'Migration and Integration at Troy from the End of the Late Bronze Age to the Iron Age', in N. Chr. Stampolidis, Ç. Maner and K. Kopanias (eds.) *Nostoi. Indigenous Culture, Migration, and Integration in the Aegean Islands and Western Anatolia during the Late Bronze Age and Early Iron Ages*, 185–210. Istanbul: Koç University Press.

Aslan, R. and M. Atabey. 2012. 'Atatürk in Troy', in J. Kelder, G. Uslu and Ö.F. Şerifoğlu (eds.) *Troy. City, Homer, Turkey*, 155–159. Istanbul: W Books.

Astour, M.J. 1965. 'New Evidence on the Last Days of Ugarit', *American Journal of Archaeology* 69.

Atabey, M., Körpe, K. and M. Erat. 2016. 'Remembering Gallipoli from a Turkish Perspective', in A. Sagona, M. Atabey, C.J. Mackie, I. McGibbon and R. Reid (eds.) *Anzac Battlefield. A Gallipoli Landscape of War and Memory*, 222–242. Cambridge: Cambridge University Press.

Atakuman, Ç. 2008. 'Cradle or Crucible? Anatolia and Archaeology in the Early Years of the Turkish Republic', *Journal of Social Archaeology* 8: 214–235.

Aubet, M.E. 2013. *Commerce and Colonization in the Ancient Near East.* Cambridge: Cambridge University Press.

Aurell, M. 2007. 'Henry II and Arthurian Legend', in C. Harper-Bill and N. Vincent (eds.) *Henry II. New Interpretation*, 362–394. Wodbridge, Suffolk: Boydell Press.

Bachhuber, C. 2011. 'Negotiating Metal and the Metal Form in the Royal Tombs of Alacahöyük in North-Central Anatolia', in Toby C. Wilkinson, E. Susan Sherratt and

John Bennet (eds.) *Interweaving Worlds. Systemic Interactions in Eurasia, 7th to 1st Millennia BC*, 158–176. Oxford: Oxbow.

Bachhuber, C. and G. Roberts (eds.) 2012. *Forces of Transformation: The End of the Bronze Age in the Mediterranean*. Oxford: Oxbow.

Bachvarova, M.R. 2015. *From Hittite to Homer. The Anatolian Background of Ancient Greek Epic*. Cambridge: Cambridge University Press.

Barjamovic, G. 2011. *A Historical Geography of Anatolia in the Old Assyrian Colony Period*. Copenhagen: Museums Tusculanum Press.

Barlow, J. 1995. 'Gregory of Tours and the Myth of the Trojan Origins of the Franks', *Frühmittelalterliche Studien* 29: 86–95.

Bass, G.F. 1987. 'Oldest Known Shipwreck Reveals Bronze Age Splendors', *National Geographic* 172.6: 693–733.

Bates, C. 2010. '*The Faerie Queene*: Britain's National Monument', in C. Bates (ed.) *The Cambridge Companion to Epic*, 133–145. Cambridge: Cambridge University Press.

Bayne, N.P. 2000. *The Grey Wares of Northwest Anatolia in the Middle and Late Bronze Age and Early Iron Age and their Relation to the Early Greek Settlements*. Asia Minor Studien 37. Bonn.

Beaune, C. 1991. *The Birth of an Ideology. Myths and Symbols of Nation in Late-Medieval France*. Berkeley: University of California Press.

Beckman, G. 1996. *Hittite Diplomatic Texts*. Atlanta: Scholars Press.

Beckman, G. 2011. 'The Hittite Language: Recovery and Grammatical Sketch', in S.R. Steadman and G. McMahon (eds.) *The Oxford Handbook of Ancient Anatolia*, 517–533. Oxford: Oxford University Press.

Beckman, G., Bryce, T. and E. Cline. 2011. *The Ahhiyawa Texts*. Atlanta: Society of Biblical Literature.

Becks, R., W. Rigter and P. Hnila. 2006. 'Das Terrassenhaus im westlichen Unterstandsviertel von Troia', *Studia Troica* 15: 99–120.

Bellinger, A.R. 1961. *Troy. The Coins*. Princeton: Princeton University Press.

Bevington, D. 1998. 'Introduction', in D. Bevington (ed.) *Troilus and Cressida. The Arden Shakespeare*, 1–117. London: Bloomsbury Publishing.

Birley, A. 1997. *Hadrian: The Restless Emperor*. London and New York: Routledge.

Blegen, C.W. 1963. *Troy and the Trojans*. New York: Frederick A. Praeger.

Blegen, C.W., J.L. Caskey M. Rawson and J. Sperling. 1950. *Troy I: The First and Second Settlements*. Princeton: Princeton University Press.

Blegen, C.W., J.L. Caskey and M. Rawson. 1951. *Troy II: The Third, Fourth and Fifth Settlements*. Princeton: Princeton University Press.

Blegen, C.W., J.L. Caskey and M. Rawson. 1953. *Troy III: The Sixth Settlement*. Princeton: Princeton University Press.

Blegen, C.W., C.G. Boulter, J.L. Caskey and M. Rawson. 1958. *Troy IV: Settlements VIIa, VIIb and VIII*. Princeton: Princeton University Press.

Blum, S. 2006. 'Troia an der Wende von der frühen zur mittleren Bronzezeit: Troia IV und Troia V', in M. Korfmann (ed.) *Troia: Archäologie eines Siedlungshügels und seine Landschaft*, 145–154. Mainz: Philipp von Zabern.

Bouet, P. 1995. 'De l'origine troyenne des Normands', *Cahier des Annales de Normandie* 26: 401–413.

Boeck, E.N. 2015. *Imagining the Byzantine Past. The Perception of History in the Illustrated Manuscripts of Skylitzes and Manasses*. Cambridge: Cambridge University Press.

Bowra, C.M. 1960. 'Homeric Epithets for Troy', *Journal of Hellenic Studies* 80: 16–23.

Briggs, J.C. 1981. 'Chapman's *Seaven Bookes of the Iliades*: Mirror for Essex', *Studies in English Literature, 1500–1700* 21: 59–73.

Brilliant, R. 2000. *My Laocoön. Alternative Claims in the Interpretation of Artworks*. Berkeley: University of California Press.

Broodbank, C. 2000. *An Island Archaeology of the Early Cyclades*. Cambridge: Cambridge University Press.

Bruckner, M.T. 2015. 'Remembering the Trojan War: Violence Past, Present and Future in Bentoît de Sainte-Maure's *Roman de Troie*', *Speculum* 90: 366–390.

Bryce, T. 2006. *The Kingdom of the Hittites*. Oxford: Oxford University Press.

Buchthal, H. 1971. *Historia Troiana. Studies in the History of Medieval Secular Illustration*. London and Leiden: The Warburg Institute and Brill.

Burgess, J.S. 2001. *The Tradition of the Trojan War in Homer and the Epic Cycle*. Baltimore, MA: John Hopkins University Press.

Burgess, J.S. 2005. 'The Epic Cycle and Its Fragments', in J.M. Foley (ed.) *A Companion to Ancient Epic*. Oxford: Wiley-Blackwell.

Burrow, C. 2013. *Shakespeare and Classical Antiquity*. Oxford: Oxford University Press.

Çakirlar, C. and R. Becks. 2009. 'Murex dye production at Troia: assessment of archaeomalacological data from old and new excavations', *Studia Troica* 18: 87–103.

Calder, W.M. 1980. 'Wilamowitz on Schliemann', *Philologus* 124: 146–151.

Cartledge, P. 1997. *The Greeks: A Portrait of Self and Others*. Oxford: Oxford University Press.

Cartledge, P. 2004. *Alexander the Great. The Hunt for a New Past*. New York: Overlook Press.

Castriota, D. 2005. 'Feminizing the Barbarian and Barbarizing the Feminine. Amazons, Trojans, and Persians in the Stoa Poikile', in J.M. Barringer and J.M. Hurwitt (eds.) *Periclean Athens and its Legacy. Problems and Perspectives*, 89–102. Austin: University of Texas Press.

Clauss, J.J. and M. Cuypers (eds.) 2010. *A Companion to Hellenistic Literature*. Oxford: Wiley-Blackwell.

Cline, E.H. 2013. *The Trojan War: A Very Short Introduction*. Oxford: Oxford University Press.

Cline. E.H. 2014. *1177 B.C. The Year That Civilization Collapsed*. Princeton: Princeton University Press.

Cohen, A. 1995. 'Alexander and Achilles – Macedonians and "Mycenaeans"', in J.B. Carter and S.P. Morris (eds.) *The Ages of Homer*, 483–505. Austin: University of Texas Press.

Colvin, S. 2010. *A Historical Greek Reader. From Mycenaean to the Koine*. Oxford: Oxford University Press.

Cornell, T.J. 1975. 'Aeneas and the Twins: The Development of the Roman Foundation Legend', *Proceedings of the Cambridge Philological Society* 21: 1–32.

Damian-Grint, P. 1999. *The New Historians of the Twelfth-Century Renaissance*. Woodbridge, Suffolk: Boydell and Brewer.

Denney, J. 2012. 'The Abduction of Helen: A Western Theme in a Chinese Embroidery of the First Half of the Seventeenth Century', *Textile Society of America Symposium Proceedings*. Paper 674.

Desmond, M. 2016. 'Trojan Itineraries and the Matter of Troy', in R. Copeland (ed.) *The Oxford History of Classical Receptions in English Literature. Volume I: 800–1558*, 251–264. Oxford: Oxford University Press.

Dickinson, O.T.P.K. 2006. *The Aegean from Bronze Age to Iron Age: Continuity and Change between the Twelfth and Eighth centuries B.C.* London and New York: Routledge.

Dougherty, C. 1994. Archaic Greek Foundation Poetry: Questions of Genre and Occasion', *Journal of Hellenic Studies* 114: 35–46.

Dörpfeld, W. 1894. *Troja 1893: Bericht über die im Jahre 1893 in Troja veranstalten Ausgrabungen*. Leipzig: F.A. Brockhaus.

Dörpfeld, W. 1902. *Troja und Ilion: Ergebnisse der Ausgrabunen in den vorhistorischen und historischen Schichten von Ilion 1870–1894*. Athens: Beck & Barth.

Düring, B.S. 2011. *The Prehistory of Asia Minor: From Complex Hunter-Gatherers to Early Urban Societies*. Cambridge: Cambridge University Press.

Easton, D.F. J.D. Hawkins, A.G. Sherratt, and E.S. Sherratt. 2002. 'Troy in Recent Perspective', *Anatolian Studies* 52: 75–109.

Edwards, M.W. 2005. 'Homer's *Iliad*', in J.M. Foley (ed.) *A Companion to Ancient Epic*, 302–314. Oxford: Wiley-Blackwell.

Eley, P. 1991. 'The Myth of Trojan Descent and Perceptions of National Identity: The Case of Eneas and the Roman de Troie', *Nottingham Medieval Studies* 35: 27–41.

Erskine, A. (ed.) 2003. *A Companion to the Hellenistic World*. Malden, MA: Blackwell.

Efe, T. 2007. 'The Theories of the "Great Caravan Route" between Cilicia and Troy: The Early Bronze Age III Period in Inland Western Anatolia', *Anatolian Studies* 57: 47–64.

Erkanal, H. 1999. 'Early Bronze Age Fortification Systems in the Izmir Region', in P.P. Betancourt, V. Karageorghis, R. Laffineur and W.-D. Niemeier (eds.) *Meletemata. Studies in Aegean Archaeology Presented to Malcom Wiener as He Enters His 65th Year [Aegaeum 20]*, 237–241. Liège/Austin, TX: Université de Liège.

Fantuzzi, M. and C. Tsagalis (eds.) 2015. *The Greek Epic Cycle and Its Reception: A Companion*. Cambridge: Cambridge University Press.

Feldman, M. 2006. *Diplomacy by Design: Luxury Arts and an 'International Style' in the Ancient Near East, 1400–1200 BCE.* Chicago: University of Chicago Press.

Fleet, K. (ed.) 2009. *The Cambridge History of Turkey. Volume I: Byzantium to Turkey 1071–1453.* Cambridge: Cambridge University Press.

Florence, M. 2004. 'The Trojan Heritage'. *The 2004 USC Football Media Guide.* USC Athletics Department. 201–209.

Flower, H.I. (ed.) 2014 (2nd edition) *The Cambridge Companion to the Roman Republic.* Cambridge: Cambridge University Press.

Foley, J.M. 1997. 'Oral Tradition and Its Implications', in I. Morris and B. Powell (eds.) *A New Companion to Homer,* 156–174. Leiden: Brill.

Foley, M.J. 2002. *How to Read an Oral Poem.* Champaign: University of Illinois Press.

Frisch, P. 1975. *Die Inschriften von Ilion.* Inschriften griechischer Städte aus Kleinasien 3. Bonn: Habelt.

Fuchs, W. 1973. 'Die Bildeschichte der Flucht des Aeneas', *ANRW* 1.4: 615–632.

Gale, N.H. (ed.) 1991. *Bronze Age Trade in the Mediterranean [SIMA 90].* Jonsered: Paul Åstroms Förlag.

Gladstone, W.E. 1958. *Studies on Homer and the Homeric Age. Volume II.* Oxford: Oxford University Press.

Goldhill, S. 1991. *The Poet's Voice. Essays on Poetics and Greek Literature.* Cambridge: Cambridge University Press.

Graziosi, B. 2002. *Inventing Homer: The Early Reception of Epic.* Cambridge: Cambridge University Press.

Graziosi, B. 2015. 'On Seeing the Poet: Arabic, Italian and Byzantine Portraits of Homer', *Scandinavian Journal of Byzantine and Modern Greek Studies* 1: 25–47.

Graziosi, B. 2016. *Homer.* Oxford: Oxford University Press.

Greaves, A.M. 2002. *Miletos. A History.* London and New York: Routledge.

Greenfield, M.A. 2000. 'Fragments of Nationalism in *Troilus and Cressida*', *Shakespeare Quarterly* 51: 171–200.

Grethlein, J. 2010. 'From Imperishable Glory to History. The *Iliad* and the Trojan War', in K. Raaflaub and D. Konstan (eds.) *Epic and History,* 122–144. London: Routledge.

Gumpert, M. 2001. *Grafting Helen. The Abduction of the Classical Past.* Madison: University of Wisconsin Press.

Gür, A. 2010. 'Political Excavations of the Anatolian Past: Nationalism and Archaeology in Turkey', in R. Boytner, L. Swartz Dodd and B.J. Parker (eds.) *Controlling the Past, Owning the Future. The Political Uses of Archaeology in the Middle East,* 68–89. Tucson: The University of Arizona Press.

Hall, E. 1989. *Inventing the Barbarian: Greek Self-Definition through Tragedy.* Oxford: Oxford University Press.

Hall, J.M. 2002. *Hellenicity: Between Ethnicity and Culture.* Chicago: University of Chicago Press.

Hammond, N.G.L. 1980. 'The Battle of the Granicus River', *Journal of Hellenic Studies* 100: 73–88.

Harper, J. 2005. 'Turks and Trojans, Trojans as Turks: Visual Imagery of the Trojan War and the Politics of Cultural Identity in Fifteenth-Century Europe', in A.J. Kabir and D. Williams (eds.) *Postcolonial Approaches to the European Middle Ages: Translating Culture*, 151–179. Cambridge: Cambridge University Press.

Haubold, J. 2013. *Greece and Mesopotamia. Dialogues in Literature*. Cambridge: Cambridge University Press.

Hawkins, J.D. 1998. 'Tarkasnawa King of Mira, "Tarkondemos", Boğazköy Sealings, and Karabel,' *Anatolian Studies* 48: 1–31.

Hering, K. 2015. 'Godfrey of Viterbo: Historical Writing and Imperial Legitimacy at the Early Hohenstaufen Court', in T. Foerster (ed.) *Godfrey pf Viterbo and His Readers. Imperial Tradition and Universal History in Late Medieval Europe*, 47–66. London and New York: Routledge.

Hertel, D. and F. Kolb. 2003. 'Troy in Clearer Perspective', *Anatolian Studies* 53: 71–88.

Heuck Allen, S. 1999. *Finding the Walls of Troy: Frank Calvert and Heinrich Schliemann at Hisarlik*. Berkeley and Los Angeles: University of California Press.

Hitchcock, L.A. and A. Maier. 2014. 'Yo-ho, Yo-hp, A Seren's Life for me!', *World Archaeology* 46: 624-640.

Hornblower, S. 2015. *Lykophron: Alexandra*. Oxford: Oxford University Press.

Isaac, B.H. 2006. *The Invention of Racism in Classical Antiquity*. Princeton: Princeton University Press.

Jablonka, P. and C.B. Rose. 2004. 'Late Bronze Age Troy: A Response to Frank Kolb', *American Journal of Archaeology* 108: 615–630.

Jablonka, P. 2010. 'Troy', in E.H. Cline (ed.) *The Oxford Handbook of the Bronze Age Aegean*, 849–861. Oxford: Oxford University Press.

Jablonka, P. 2011. 'Troy in Regional and International Context', in S.R. Steadman and G. McMahon (eds.) *The Oxford Handbook of Ancient Anatolia*, 717–733. Oxford: Oxford University Press.

Jansen, H.G. and N. Blindow. 2003. 'The Geophysical Mapping of the Lower City of Troia/Ilion', in G.A. Wagner, E. Pernicka and H.-P. Uerpmann (eds.) *Troia and the Troad. Scientific Approaches*, 325–340. Berlin: Springer.

Jeffery, L.H. 1961 (see 2003 revised edition). *The Local Scripts of Archaic Greece*. Oxford: Oxford University Press.

Johnstone, S. 2014. 'A New History of Libraries and Books in the Hellenistic Period', *Classical Antiquity* 33: 347–393.

Kim, H.J. 2009. *Ethnicity and Foreigners in Ancient Greece and China*. London: Duckworth.

Kolb, F. 2004. 'Troy VI: A Trading Center and Commercial City?' *American Journal of Archaeology* 108: 577–613.

Kolb, F. 2010. *Tatort 'Troia': Geschichte, Mythen, Politik*. Munich: Ferdinand Schöningh.

Koerner, B. 2006. 'The Other Trojan War. What's the Bestselling Condom in America?' *The Slate*, 29 September.

Korfmann, M. 1997. *A Guide to Troia*. Istanbul: Ege Yayınları.

Korfmann, M. 2000. 'Troia: Ausgrabungen 1999', *Studia Troica* 10: 1–52.

Korfmann, M. 2001. 'Troia/Wilusa – Ausgrabunden 2000', *Studia Troica* 11: 1–50.

Korfmann, M. 2004. 'Was There a Trojan War?', *Archaeology* 57.3: 37.

Kouka, O. 2013. '"Minding the Gap". Against the Gaps: The Early Bronze Age and the Transition to the Middle Bronze Age in the Northern and Eastern Aegean/Western Anatolia', *American Journal of Archaeology* 117: 569–580.

Kouklanakis, A. 2016. 'From Cultural Appropriation to Historical Emendation: Two Case Studies of Receptions of the Classical Tradition in Brazil', in E. Rizo and M.M. Henry (eds.) *Receptions of the Classics in the African Diaspora of the Hispanophone and Lusophone Worlds*, 9–30. Lanham, MD: Lexington Books.

Krevans, N. 2000. 'On the Margins of Epic: The Foundation-Poems of Apollonius', in M.A. Harder, R.F. Regtuit and G.C. Wakker (eds.) *Hellenistica Groningana. 4. Apollonius Rhodius*, 69–84. Louvain: Peeters.

Laffineur, R. and E. Greco (eds.) 2005. *Emporia. Aegeans in the Central and Eastern Mediterranean. Aegaeum 25*. Austin/Liege: University of Liege.

Landmann, J. 1998. *Troia Negra: a Saga dos Palmares*. São Paulo: Editora Mandarim.

Langgut, D., I. Finkelstein and L. Thomas. 2013. 'Climate and the Late Bronze Collapse: New Evidence from the Southern Levant', *Journal of Institute of Archaeology of Tel Aviv University* 40: 149–175.

Latacz, J. 2004. *Troy and Homer. Towards a Solution to an Old Mystery*. Oxford: Oxford University Press.

Lateiner, D. 2004. 'The *Iliad*: An Unpredictable Classic', in R. Fowler (ed.) *The Cambridge Companion to Homer*, 11–30. Cambridge: Cambridge University Press.

Lloyd, S. and J. Mellaart 1965. *Beycesultan I. The Chalcolithic and Early Bronze Levels*. London: British Institute at Ankara.

Lowenstam, S. 2008. *As Witnessed by Images: The Trojan War Tradition in Greek and Etruscan Art*. Baltimore, MA: John Hopkins University Press.

Macedo, S.D.T. 1963. *Palmares: A Troia Negra*. São Paulo: São Paulo Editora.

Mac Sweeney, N. 2010. 'Hittites and Arzawans: A view from western Anatolia', *Anatolian Studies* 60: 7–24.

Maguire, L. 2009. *Helen of Troy. From Homer to Hollywood*. London and New York: Wiley-Blackwell.

Malkin, I. 1998. *The Returns of Odysseus: Colonization and Ethnicity*. Berkeley: University of California Press.

Malkin, I. 2011. *A Small Greek World: Networks in the Ancient Mediterranean*. Oxford and New York: Oxford University Press.

Manning, S.W. and I. Hulin. 2005. 'Maritime Commerce and Geographies of Mobility in the Late Bronze Age of the eastern Mediterranean: Problematizations', in A.B. Knapp and E. blake (eds.) *The Archaeology of Mediterranean Prehistory*, 270–302. Malden: Blackwell.

Meserve, M. 2008. *Empires of Islam in Renaissance Historical Thought*. Cambridge, MA: Harvard University Press.

Maran, J. and P.W. Stockhammer (eds.) 2012. *Materiality and Social Practice: Transformative Capacities of Intercultural Encounters*. Oxford: Oxbow.

Michel, C. 2001. *Correspondance des marchands de Kaniš au début du IIe millénaire av. J.-C. Littératures du Proche-Orient ancien 19*. Paris: Éditions du Cerf.

Midford, S. 2010. 'From Achilles to Anzac: Heroism in The Dardanelles from Antiquity to the Great War', Australasian Society for Classical Studies 31, Conference Proceedings.

Midford, S. 2013. 'Anzacs and the Heroes of Troy: Exploring the Universality of War in Sidney Nolan's "Gallipoli Series"', in I. Güran Yumsak and M. Mehdi Ilhan (eds.) *Gallipoli: History, Legend and Memory [Gelibolou: Tarih, Esfane ve Ani]*, 303–312. Istanbul: Istanbul Medeniyet University Press.

Mitchell, L.G. 2007. *Panhellenism and the Barbarian in Archaic and Classical Greece*. Swansea: Classical Press of Wales.

Moran, W.L. 2000. *The Amarna Letters*. Baltimore: John Hopkins University Press.

Morris, S. 1989. 'A Tale of Two Cities: The Miniature Frescoes from Thera and the Origins of Greek Poetry', *American Journal of Archaeology* 93: 511–535.

Muhly, James. 2011. 'Metals and Metallurgy', in S.R. Steadman and G. McMahon (eds.) *The Oxford Handbook of Ancient Anatolia (10,000–323 BCE)*, 858–876. Oxford: Oxford University Press.

Nicoll, A. 1998. 'Introduction', in A. Nicoll (ed.) *Chapman's Homer: The Iliad. Translated into English by George Chapman*. Princeton: Princeton University Press.

Nuttall, A.D. 2004. 'Action at a Distance: Shakespeare and the Greeks', in C. Martindale and A.B. Taylor (eds.) *Shakespeare and the Classics*, 209–222. Cambridge: Cambridge University Press.

Osborne, R. 2009. *Greece in the Making, 1200–479 BC [2nd edition]*. London and New York: Routledge.

Özgüç, T. 2003. *Kültepe Kaniš/Neša. The Earliest International Trade Center and the Oldest Capital City of the Hittites*. Tokyo–Istanbul: Middle East Culture Centre in Japan.

Palaima, T.G. 2010. 'Linear B', in *The Oxford Handbook of the Bronze Age Aegean*, 356–372. Oxford: Oxford University Press.

Pantazis, V.D. 2009. 'Wilusa: Reconsidering the Evidence,' *Klio* 91: 291–310.

Paul, J. 2013. *Film and the Classical Epic Tradition*. Oxford: Oxford University Press.

Pavúk, P. 2010. 'Minyan or Not: The Second Millennium Grey Ware in Western Anatolia and Its Relation to Mainland Greece', in A. Philippa-Touchias, G. Touchias, S. Voutsaki and J.C. Wright (ed.) *Mesohelladika: La Grèce continentale au Bronze Moyen*, 931–943. Athens: BCH Supplement.

Pavúk, P. 2012. 'Of Spools and Discoid Loomweights: Aegean-Type Weaving at Troy Revisited', in M.-L. Nosch and R. Laffineur (eds.) *Kosmos. Jewellery, Adornment and Textiles in the Aegean Bronze Age. Aegaeum 33*, 121–130. Leuven-Liege: Peeters.

Pertz, G.H. 1844. *Monumenta Germanicae Historica. Tomus VI.* Hannover: Impensis Bibliopolii Aulici Hahniani.

Powell, B. 1997. 'Homer and Writing', in I. Morris and B. Powell (eds.) *A New Companion to Homer*, 3–32. Leiden: Brill.

Pryor, J.H. 2015. 'A Medieval Siege of Troy: The Fight to the Death at Acre, 1189–1192 or the tears of Salah al-Din', in G.I. Halford (ed.) *The Medieval Way of War. Studies in Medieval Military History in Honour of Bernard S. Bachrach*, 97–115. London and New York: Routledge.

Pulak, C. 1998. 'The Uluburun Shipwreck: An Overview.' *International Journal of Nautical Archaeology* 27, 188–224.

Rabeyroux, A. 1992. 'Images de la "merveille": la "Chambre de Beautés"', *Médiévales* 11: 31–45.

Riggs, C.T. 1954. *History of Mehmed the Conqueror, by Kritovoulos, translated by C.T. Riggs*. Princeton: Princeton University Press.

Riorden, E.H. 2014. 'Conservation and Presentation at the Site of Troy, 1988–2008', in E. Pernicka, C.B. Rose and P. Jablonka (eds.) *Troia 1987–2012: Grabungen un Forschungen I: Forschungungsgeschichte, Methoden und Landschaft*, 428–451. Bonn: Rudolph Habelt.

Roller, L.E. 1999. *In Search of God the Mother. The Cult of Anatolian Cybele*. Berkeley: University of California Press.

Rose, C.B. 2014. *The Archaeology of Greek and Roman Troy*. Cambridge: Cambridge University Press.

Rose, C.B. and R. Körpe. 2016. 'The Tumuli of Troy and the Troad', in O. Henry and U. Kelp (eds.) *Tumuli as Sema. Space, Politics, Culture and Religion in the First Milenniums BC*, 373–386. Berlin: Walter de Gruyter.

Rossi, A. 2001. 'Remapping the Past: Caesar's Tale of Troy (Lucan "BC" 9.964-999)', *Pheonix* 55: 313–326.

Said, E. 1978 [reprinted in 1995 with a new Afterword]. *Orientalism*. London: Keegan Paul and Routledge.

Sagona, A. and P. Zimansky 2009. *Ancient Turkey*. Abingdon: Routledge.

Şahin, H. 2004. *Troyalılar Türk müydü? Mir Mitos'un Dünü, Bugünü ve Yarını* (Were the Trojans Truks? Past, Present, and Future of a Mythos).

Şahoğlu, V. 2005. 'The *Anatolian Trade Network* and the Izmir Region during the Early Bronze Age', *Oxford Journal of Archaeology* 24: 339–361.

Sazcı, G. 2001. 'Gebäude mit vermutlich kultischer Funktion. Das Megaron in Quadrat G6', in *Troia. Traum und Wirklichkeit*, 382–390. Stuttgart: Konrad Theiss Verlag.

Sazcı, G. 2005. 'Troia I–III, die Maritime und Troia IV–V, die Anatolische Troia-Kultur: eine Untersuchung der Funde und Befunde im mittleren Schliemanngraben (D07, D08)', *Studia Troica* 15: 33–98.

Scheer, T. 2003. 'The Past in a Hellenistic Present: Myth and Local Tradition', in A. Erskine (ed.) *A Companion to the Hellenistic World*, 216–231. Oxford: Wiley-Blackwell.

Schein, S. 1996. 'The *Iliad*: Structure and Interpretation', in I. Morris and B. Powell (eds.) *A New Companion to Homer*, 345–359. Leiden: Brill.

Schein, S. forthcoming. 'The *Iliad* as Prince's Mirror in Chapman's Translation and Shakespeare's *Troilus and Cressida*', in J. J. H. Klooster and B. van den Berg (eds.), *Homer and the Good Ruler. The Reception of Homeric Epic as Princes' Mirror through the Ages*. Leiden: Brill.

Schliemann, H. 1874. *Trojanischer Alterthümer. Bericht über die Ausgrabungen in Troja*. Leipzig: F.A. Brockhaus:.

Schliemann, H. 1875. *Troy and its Remains. A Narrative of the Researches and Discoveries Made on the Site of Ilium, and in the Trojan Plain (edited by Philip Smith)*. London: John Murray.

Schliemann, H. 1880. *Ilios: The City and Country of the Trojans*. London: John Murray.

Schliemann, H. 1884. *Troja: Results of the Latest Researches and Discoveries on the Site of Homer's Troy and in the Heroic Tumuli and Other Sites, Made in the Year 1882*. New York: Harper and Brothers.

Scully, S. 1991. *Homer and the Sacred City*. Ithaca, NY: Cornell University Press.

Séfériadès, M. 1985. *Troie I. Matériaux pour l'étude des societes du nord-est Égéen au debut du Bronze Ancien*. Paris: Éditions Recherche sur les Civilisations.

Seferis, G. 1995. *George Seferis. Collected Poems. Translated, Edited and Introduced by Edmund Keeley and Philip Sherrard*. Princeton: Princeton University Press.

Shawcross, T. 2003. 'Re-inventing the Homeland in the Historiography of Frankish Greece: The Fourth Crusade and the Legend of the Trojan War', *Byzantine and Modern Greek Studies* 27: 120–152.

Shepard, A. and D. Powell (eds.) 2004. *Fantasies of Troy. Classical Tales and the Social Imaginary in Medieval and Early Modern Europe*. Toronto: Centre for Reformation and Renaissance Studies.

Sherratt, E.S. 1990. '"Reading the Texts": Archaeology and the Homeric Question', *Antiquity* 64: 807–824.

Sherratt, A. and S. Sherratt. 1993. 'The Growth of the Mediterranean Economy in the Early First Millennium BC', *World Archaeology* 24: 361–378.

Shipley, G. 1999. *The Greek World After Alexander, 323–30 BCE*. London and New York: Routledge.

Skinner, J. 2012. *The Invention of Greek Ethnography from Homer to Herodotus*. Oxford: Oxford University Press.

Solomon, J. 2015. 'Homer's *Iliad* in Popular Culture: The Roads to *Troy*', in M.M. Winkler (ed.) *Return to* Troy. *New Essays on the Hollywood Epic*, 224–254. Leiden: Brill.

Sowerby, R. 1992. 'Chapman's Discovery of Homer', *Translation and Literature* 1: 26–51.

Squire, M. 2011. *The iliad in a Nutshell: Visualizing epic on the Tabulae Iliacae*. Oxford: Oxford University Press.

Squire, M. 2015. 'Figuring Rome's Foundation on the Iliac Tables', in N. Mac Sweeney (ed.) *Foundation Myths in Ancient Societies: Dialogues and Discourses*, 151–189. Philadelphia: University of Pennsylvania Press.

Stark, J. 1984. 'After 20 Years Awash with Booze and Drugs, Troy Donahue Prizes his Sobering Discoveries', *People Magazine*, 13 August 1984.

Starke, F. 1997. 'Troia in Kontext des historisch-politischen Umfeldes Kleinasien im 2. Jarhtausend', *Studia Troica* 7: 447–487.

Steadman, S.R. 2011. 'The Early Bronze Age on the Plateau', in S.R. Steadman and G. McMahon (eds.) *The Oxford Handbook of Ancient Anatolia (10,000–323 BCE)*, 229–259. Oxford: Oxford University Press.

Stones, A. 2005. 'Seeing the walls of Troy', in B. Dekeyzer and J. van den Stock (eds.) *Manuscripts in Transition: Recycling Manuscripts, Texts and Images*, 161–178. Louvain: Peeters.

Sullivan, P. 1985. 'Medieval Automata: The "Chambre de Beautés" in Bentoît's Roman de Troie', *Romance Studies* 3: 1–20.

Summers, R.C. 1999. *Secure Computing: Threats and Safeguards*. Maidenhead: McGraw Hill.

Tanner, M. 1993. *The Last Descendant of Aeneas. The Habsburgs and the Mythic Image of the Emperor*. New Haven: Yale University Press.

Thomas, R. 1992. *Literacy and Orality in Ancient Greece*. Cambridge: Cambridge University Press.

Thomas, R. 2001. *Herodotus in context. Ethnography, Science, and the Art of Persuasion*. Cambridge: Cambridge University Press.

Tone, A. 2002. *Devices and Desires. A History of Contraceptives in America*. New York: Hill and Wang.

Traill, D.A. 1995. *Schliemann of Troy: Treasure and Deceit*. New York: St Martin's Press.

Treichler, P.A. 2014. '"When Pirates Feast … Who Pays?" Condoms, Advertising, and the Visibility Paradox, 1920s and 1930s', *Journal of Bioethical Enquiry* 11: 479–505.

Uslu, G. 2012. 'Homer and Troy in 19th Century Ottoman Turkish Literature', in J. Kelder, G. Uslu and Ö.F. Şerifoğlu (eds.) *Troy. City, Homer, Turkey*, 143–149. Istanbul: W Books.

Vaio, J. 1992. 'Gladstone and the Early Reception of Schliemann in England', in W.M. Calder and J. Cober (eds.) *Heinrich Schliemann nach hundert Jahren*. Frankfurt: Vittorio Klostermann.

Van de Mieroop, M. 2007 (2nd edition). *A History of the Ancient Near East ca. 3000–323 BC*. London and New York: Routledge.

Vandiver, E. 2010. *Stand in the Trench, Achilles. Classical Receptions in British Poetry of the Great War*. Oxford: Oxford University Press.

Vansina, J. 1985. *Oral Tradition as History*. Madison, WI: University of Wisconsin Press.

Veenhof, K.R. 2000. 'Trade and Politics in Ancient Assur. Balancing of Public, Colonial and Entrepreneurial Interests', in C. Zaccagnini (ed.) *Mercanti e politica nel mondo antico*, 69–118. Rome: Bretschneider.

Veenhof, K.R. 2013. 'The Archives of Old Assyrian Traders: their Nature, Functions and Use', in M. Faraguna (ed.) *Archives and Archival Documents in Ancient Societies: Legal Documents in Ancient Societies IV*, 27–62. Trieste: EUT Edizioni Università di Trieste.

Weaver, E.B. 2007. 'Gender', in G. Ruggiero (ed.) *A Companion to the Worlds of the Renaissance*, 188–207. Oxford: Wiley-Blackwell.

Webb, P.A. 1996. *Hellenistic Architectural Sculpture: Figural Motifs in Western Anatolia and the Aegean Islands*. Madison: University of Wisconsin Press.

West, M.L. 1993. *Greek Lyric Poetry*. Oxford: Oxford University Press.

West, M.L. 1997. *The East Face of Helicon: West Asiatic Elements in Greek Poetry and Myth*. Oxford: Oxford University Press.

West, M.L. 2013. *The Epic Cycle: A Commentary on the Lost Troy Epics*. Oxford: Oxford University Press.

Wilamowitz-Moellendorff, U. von. 1884. *Homerische Untersuchungen*. Berlin: Weidmann.

Wilamowitz-Moellendorff, U. von. 1916. *Die Ilias und Homer*. Berlin: Weidmannsche Buchhandlung.

Winkler, M.M. (ed.) 2007. *Troy: From Homer's Iliad to Hollywood Epic*. Malden, MA: Blackwell.

Wiseman, T.P. 1995. *Remus: A Roman Myth*. Cambridge: Cambridge University Press.

Woodford, S. 1993. *The Trojan War in Ancient Art*. Ithaca, NY: Cornell University Press.

Yost, J.R. 2013. 'An Interview with Daniel J. Edwards', Charles Babbage Institute. Accessed online on 03/10/2016 at: http://conservancy.umn.edu/handle/11299/162379.

Young, A.M. 1948. *Troy and Her Legend*. Pittsburgh: University of Pittsburgh Press.

# Index

Note: The letters 'Fig.' and 'n' following locators refer to figures and note numbers respectively.